Contents

Introduction

About Unit 1

Unit 1 is worth 50 per cent of your AS level. It requires detailed knowledge of a historical period and the ability to explain the causes, consequences and significance of historical events. There are no sources in the Unit 1 exam and therefore all marks available are awarded for use of your own knowledge.

In the exam, you are required to answer two questions from a range of options. The questions are all worth 30 marks and therefore you should divide your time – including any extra time you have been allocated – equally between the questions.

The questions you answer must be on different topics. This book deals exclusively with topic F7: From Second Reich to Third Reich: Germany, 1918–1945. However, you must also be prepared to answer a question on another topic.

The exam will test your ability to:

- select information that focuses on the question
- organise this information to provide an answer to the question
- show range and depth in the examples you provide
- analyse the significance of the information used to reach an overall judgement.

From Second Reich to Third Reich: Germany, 1918–1945

The exam board specifies that students should study four general areas as part of this topic.

1. The fall of the Second Reich and the establishment of the Weimar Republic: threats from extremes of left and right; the economy; Stresemann as chancellor and foreign minister.
2. The rise of the Third Reich: formation of Nazi Party; reasons for support and opposition to the Nazis.
3. The Third Reich in action: Nazi economic solutions; *Volksgemeinschaft* (People's Community) and Nazi social policies – racial policies, minorities, treatment of Jews, women, children and education.
4. The fall of the Third Reich: impact of the Second World War on Germany and reasons for defeat.

How to use this book

This book has been designed to help you to develop the knowledge and skills necessary to succeed in the exam. The book is divided into four sections – one for each general area of the course. Each section is made up of a series of topics organised into double-page spreads. On the left-hand page, you will find a summary of the key content you need to learn. Words in bold in the key content are defined in the glossary. On the right-hand page, you will find exam-focused activities. Together, these two strands of the book will take you through the knowledge and skills essential for exam success.

my revision notes

AS Edexcel History

FROM SECOND REICH TO THIRD REICH

GERMANY, 1918–1945

Barbara Warnock

Series editors:
Robin Bunce
Laura Gallagher

HODDER EDUCATION
AN HACHETTE UK COMPANY

Every effort has been made to trace all copyright holders, but if any have been inadvertently overlooked the Publishers will be pleased to make the necessary arrangements at the first opportunity.

Although every effort has been made to ensure that website addresses are correct at time of going to press, Hodder Education cannot be held responsible for the content of any website mentioned in this book. It is sometimes possible to find a relocated web page by typing in the address of the home page for a website in the URL window of your browser.

Hachette UK's policy is to use papers that are natural, renewable and recyclable products and made from wood grown in sustainable forests. The logging and manufacturing processes are expected to conform to the environmental regulations of the country of origin.

Orders: please contact Bookpoint Ltd, 130 Milton Park, Abingdon, Oxon OX14 4SB.
Telephone: +44 (0)1235 827720. Fax: +44 (0)1235 400454. Lines are open 9.00a.m.–5.00p.m., Monday to Saturday, with a 24-hour message answering service. Visit our website at www.hoddereducation.co.uk

First published in 2014 by
Hodder Education,
An Hachette UK Company
338 Euston Road
London NW1 3BH

Impression number	10	9	8	7	6	5	4	3	2	1	
Year	2018	2017	2016	2015	2014						

Illustrations by Datapage (India) Pvt. Ltd
Typeset in 11/13 Stemple Schneidler Std–Light by Datapage (India) Pvt. Ltd
Printed in India
A catalogue record for this title is available from the British Library
ISBN 978 1 444 1 9959 8

▼ Key historical content

▼ Exam-focused activities

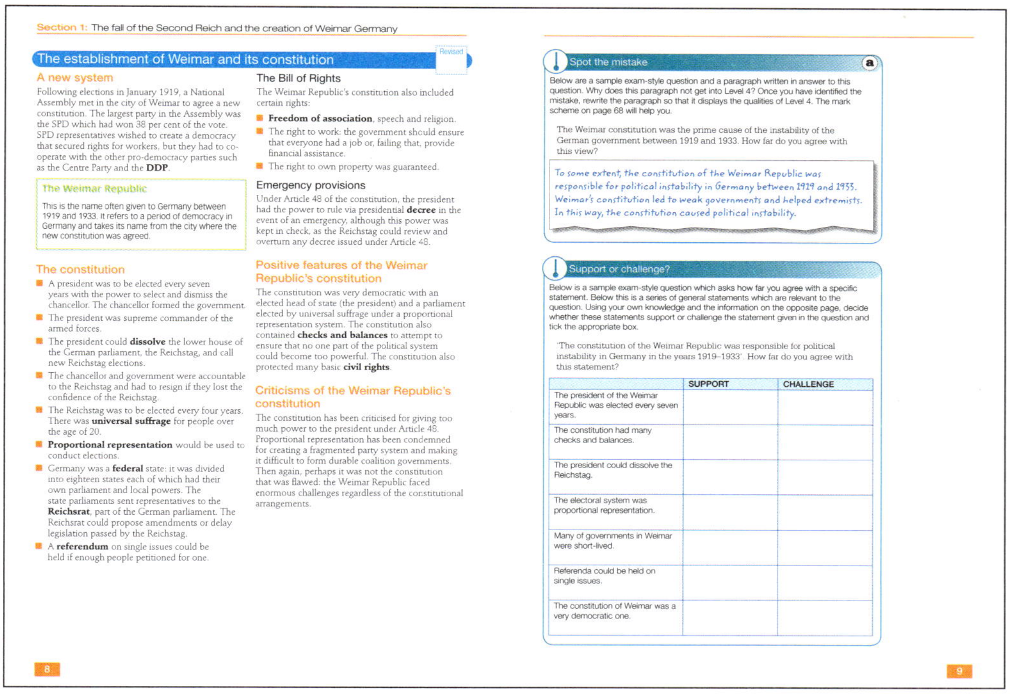

Section 1: The fall of the Second Reich and the creation of Weimar Germany

The establishment of Weimar and its constitution

Revised

A new system

Following elections in January 1919, a National Assembly met in the city of Weimar to agree a new constitution. The largest party in the Assembly was the SPD which had won 38 per cent of the vote. SPD representatives wished to create a democracy that secured rights for workers, but they had to co-operate with the other pro-democracy parties such as the Centre Party and the **DDP**.

The Weimar Republic

This is the name often given to Germany between 1919 and 1933. It refers to a period of democracy in Germany and takes its name from the city where the new constitution was agreed.

The constitution

- A president was to be elected every seven years with the power to select and dismiss the chancellor. The chancellor formed the government.
- The president was supreme commander of the armed forces.
- The president could **dissolve** the lower house of the German parliament, the Reichstag, and call new Reichstag elections.
- The chancellor and government were accountable to the Reichstag and had to resign if they lost the confidence of the Reichstag.
- The Reichstag was to be elected every four years. There was **universal suffrage** for people over the age of 20.
- **Proportional representation** would be used to conduct elections.
- Germany was a **federal** state: it was divided into eighteen states each of which had their own parliament and local powers. The state parliaments sent representatives to the **Reichsrat**, part of the German parliament. The Reichsrat could propose amendments or delay legislation passed by the Reichstag.
- A **referendum** on single issues could be held if enough people petitioned for one.

The Bill of Rights

The Weimar Republic's constitution also included certain rights:

- **Freedom of association**, speech and religion.
- The right to work: the government should ensure that everyone had a job or, failing that, provide financial assistance.
- The right to own property was guaranteed.

Emergency provisions

Under Article 48 of the constitution, the president had the power to rule via presidential **decree** in the event of an emergency, although this power was kept in check, as the Reichstag could review and overturn any decree issued under Article 48.

Positive features of the Weimar Republic's constitution

The constitution was very democratic with an elected head of state (the president) and a parliament elected by universal suffrage under a proportional representation system. The constitution also contained **checks and balances** to attempt to ensure that no one part of the political system could become too powerful. The constitution also protected many basic **civil rights**.

Criticisms of the Weimar Republic's constitution

The constitution has been criticised for giving too much power to the president under Article 48. Proportional representation has been condemned for creating a fragmented party system and making it difficult to form durable coalition governments. Then again, perhaps it was not the constitution that was flawed: the Weimar Republic faced enormous challenges regardless of the constitutional arrangements.

8

Spot the mistake

a

Below are a sample exam-style question and a paragraph written in answer to this question. Why does this paragraph not get into Level 4? Once you have identified the mistake, rewrite the paragraph so that it displays the qualities of Level 4. The mark scheme on page 68 will help you.

The Weimar constitution was the prime cause of the instability of the German government between 1919 and 1933. How far do you agree with this view?

To some extent, the constitution of the Weimar Republic was responsible for political instability in Germany between 1919 and 1933. Weimar's constitution led to weak governments and helped extremists. In this way, the constitution caused political instability.

Support or challenge?

Below is a sample exam-style question which asks how far you agree with a specific statement. Below this is a series of general statements which are relevant to the question. Using your own knowledge and the information on the opposite page, decide whether these statements support or challenge the statement given in the question and tick the appropriate box.

'The constitution of the Weimar Republic was responsible for political instability in Germany in the years 1919–1933'. How far do you agree with this statement?

	SUPPORT	CHALLENGE
The president of the Weimar Republic was elected every seven years.		
The constitution had many checks and balances.		
The president could dissolve the Reichstag.		
The electoral system was proportional representation.		
Many of governments in Weimar were short-lived.		
Referenda could be held on single issues.		
The constitution of Weimar was a very democratic one.		

9

There are three levels of exam-focused activities.

- Band 1 activities are designed to develop the foundational skills needed to pass the exam. These have a turquoise heading and this symbol:

- Band 2 activities are designed to build on the skills developed in Band 1 activities and to help you to develop the skills necessary for a C grade. These have an orange heading and this symbol:

- Band 3 activities are designed to enable you to access the highest grades. These have a purple heading and this symbol:

Some of the activities have answers or suggested answers on pages 65–67 and have the following symbol to indicate this:

Each section ends with an exam-style question and model A-grade answer with examiner's commentary. This should give you guidance on what is required to achieve the top grades.

You can also keep track of your revision by ticking off each topic heading in the book, or by ticking the checklist on the contents page. Tick each box when you have:

- revised and understood a topic
- completed the activities.

Section 1:
The fall of the Second Reich and the creation of Weimar Germany

The Second Reich 1918

Revised

The Second Reich is the name given to the unified German state that was established following **Prussia's** victory in the Franco-Prussian War 1870–1871. Following the war, all German-speaking states, with the exception of the Austrian Empire, unified under Prussian dominance. The Prussian king was Emperor or Kaiser of Germany.

The **constitution** of the Second Reich gave substantial powers of **patronage** to the Kaiser, although the agreement of the elected parliament, or **Reichstag**, was needed to pass **legislation**. The Kaiser was in charge of foreign policy and commander-in-chief of the German armed forces. Kaiser Wilhelm II, who ruled from 1888–1918, wanted to develop a German empire and build up German military strength.

In the years prior to the First World War, Germany industrialised rapidly and the urban **working class** grew substantially. A large trade union movement developed and German politics came under increasing strain as a permanently upper class, **conservative** government struggled to work with an increasingly working class, **socialist** Reichstag.

The impact of the First World War (1914–1918) on Germany

The economic impact of the war

Fighting the war was an enormous economic challenge. Taxation contributed only 16 per cent of the cost of the war. **War bonds** were also used and money printed. Printing money led to **inflation** (see page 14): the **mark** declined in value by 75 per cent between 1913 and 1918. German agriculture was not **mobilised** effectively, causing food shortages.

The social impact of the war

The impact of the war on ordinary people was often severe. Two million soldiers were killed and 6.3 million were injured. With inflation and tight controls on wages, living standards fell by 20–30 per cent. Food and fuel shortages exacerbated the impact of the **Spanish flu pandemic** in 1918 and caused misery, disease and even starvation.

The political impact of the war

At the start of the war, Germany appeared politically unified behind the war effort. A political truce or ***Burgfrieden*** was announced. This situation did not last, however:

- During the war, the government became increasingly authoritarian and militaristic. By 1916, the Supreme Commanders, Generals Hindenburg and Ludendorff were essentially in charge of the country, running what has been characterised as a 'silent dictatorship'. Military government exacerbated political and social tensions.
- Mounting concern about the war led, in 1917, to a Reichstag vote for the 'peace resolution', which urged the government to try to negotiate a peace settlement. The war also saw the formation in 1915 of the communist **Spartacist League** that agitated for **social revolution** and an end to the war. Additionally, in 1917, 42 **SPD** deputies had broken away to form the anti-war and radical socialist **USPD**.
- Discontent with the political and social situation in Germany was revealed by the huge strikes that occurred in 1917 and 1918.

By 1918, politics was more **polarised** than ever as the Generals continued to seek a ***Siegfried***, victory peace.

The impact of impending defeat

In the autumn of 1918, Germany's impending defeat came as a great shock to many Germans. This contributed to the outbreak of revolution and the acceptance of the **'stab in the back' myth**.

Mind map

Use the information on the opposite page to add detail to the mind map below.

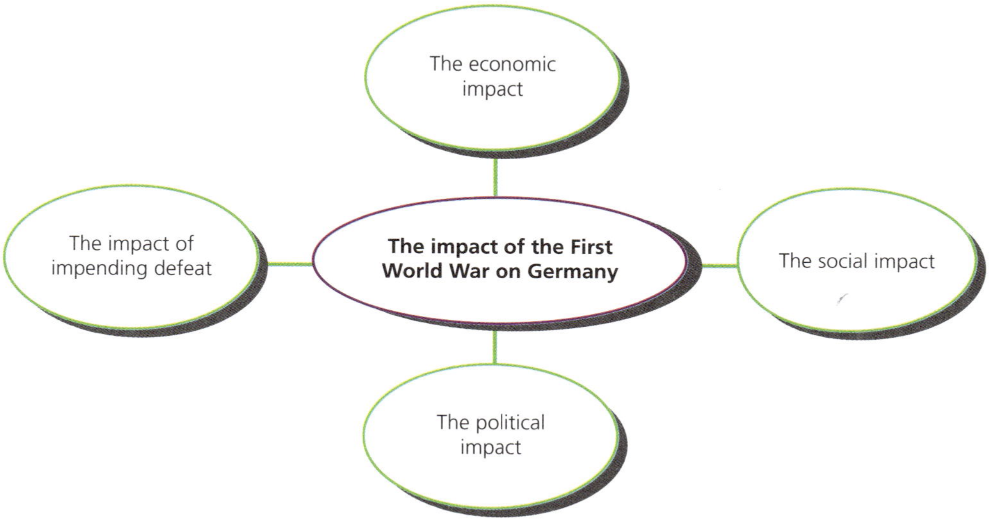

Complete the paragraph

Below are a sample exam question and a paragraph written in answer to this question. The paragraph contains a point and specific examples, but lacks a concluding explanatory link back to the question. Complete the paragraph adding this link in the space provided.

How far do you agree that the main impact of the First World War on Germany was increased political tension?

To some extent the main impact of the First World War was the political problems the war produced. The war increased tensions as many people disliked the 'silent dictatorship' of Ludendorff and Hindenburg. These generals effectively ran the country from 1916, and their authoritarian leadership produced opposition. Huge strikes in 1917 and 1918 show the extent of people's discontent. As the war dragged on, politics became more divided. The Reichstag opposed the government by urging them to try to negotiate a peace settlement in 1917, whilst the Spartacists and the USPD were completely anti-war. Politics was polarised as the generals continued to seek a Siegfried.

____

____

____

The German revolution

Revised

Causes

The Second Reich began to collapse in the final weeks of the war. A number of factors caused the 'German revolution':

The problems of the Second Reich

The political system of the Second Reich had ceased to work effectively in the years before 1914 and the start of the First World War. The tension between a permanently conservative government headed by an **autocratic** Kaiser and a growing working class with socialist inclinations made revolution in Germany more likely.

The impact of the war

The First World War had placed enormous strains on Germany as it caused escalating inflation, declining standards of living and increased political polarisation. The country had started the war reasonably united, but by the end of the war social and political tensions had pushed the system to breaking point.

The impact of impending defeat

Having defeated Russia in 1917, by the summer of 1918 the German army had appeared to be in a strong position in France and Germany but in reality were exhausted and overstretched. Foreseeing defeat, the generals sought to rid themselves of responsibility, by engineering the 'revolution from above' (see table below). When it became clear that Germany was about to surrender, German troops were still stationed inside France and Belgium. The shock caused by approaching defeat triggered widespread discontent and mutinies: the 'revolution from below'.

The German Revolution 1918–1919

Key event	Description
The revolution from above 29 September–3 October 1918	Realising that defeat was certain, the generals advised Kaiser Wilhelm to negotiate an **armistice** and form a new civilian government containing members of the Reichstag. On 3 October, the liberal Prince Max of Baden formed a new government containing liberal and socialist members of the Reichstag.
The revolution from below 31 October–8 November 1918	As realisation of impending defeat spread, sailors in Kiel, a port in northern Germany, mutinied against an order to put to sea. The mutiny soon spread to other ports and many other parts of Germany. Inspired by the mutiny, **soviets** sprung up across the country and there were riots and disturbances across Germany. The government had lost control.
The abdication of the Kaiser and the declaration of a republic 9 November 1918	Fearing a violent revolution and with the SPD calling for a republic, Hindenburg advised the Kaiser to abdicate. The Kaiser fled to Holland: the Second Reich was at an end and Friedrich Ebert, leader of the SPD, was now leader of Germany. He formed a government of SPD and USPD members.
Armistice 11 November 1918	The new government signed an armistice agreement with the **Allies**.
The limited revolution 10 November 1918–January 1919	Ebert was anti-communist and determined to prevent the German revolution becoming a civil war. He thus did a deal with the army to gain their support (the Ebert–Groener Pact: General Groener was now head of the army) and called for early democratic elections.

The nature of the German revolution

The revolution brought democracy to Germany and ended the monarchy. The government was now drawn from the Reichstag. The revolution did not, however, remove the old **aristocratic elite** from other positions of power, such as in the army and **judiciary**.

Delete as applicable

a

Below are a sample exam-style question and a paragraph written in answer to this question. Read the paragraph and decide which of the possible options (underlined) is the most appropriate. Delete the least appropriate options and complete the paragraph by justifying your selection.

To what extent was the First World War responsible for the collapse of the Second Reich in autumn 1918?

The Second Reich collapsed partially/mainly/entirely because of the impact of the First World War. The war placed enormous strains on Germany that made revolution a slight possibility/more likely/certain. For example, the cost of fighting the war led to inflation: the mark declined in value by 75 per cent during the war. Inflation and shortages reduced living standards, increased ordinary people's discontent, and made revolution more likely. In addition, the war increased political tension, with some groups such as the Spartacists and USPD opposed to Germany continuing to fight in the war. The difficulties that fighting in the First World War produced partially/mainly/entirely caused the Second Reich to collapse because

Eliminate irrelevance

a

Below are a sample exam-style question and a paragraph written in answer to this question. Read the paragraph and identify parts of the paragraph that are not directly relevant or helpful to the question. Draw a line through the information that is irrelevant and justify your deletions in the margin.

How far did the collapse of the Second Reich in autumn 1918 only occur because Germany was losing the First World War?

It is unlikely that the Second Reich would have collapsed if Germany had not been losing the First World War in autumn 1918. The revolution, which caused the Kaiser to flee and the Reich to end, was triggered by a mutiny by sailors in Kiel. The Kaiser was the supreme ruler of Germany. He took over ruling Germany in 1888 and he was very interested in ships. The sailors rebelled because they were aware that Germany was on the verge of losing the war. The political changes that had started right before the revolution were also caused by Germany losing the war, as it was this knowledge that caused the generals who were running the country to hand over power to a new government that was backed by the Reichstag. While there were underlying problems and conflicts in the Second Reich that made revolution more likely, it is still unlikely that the system would have collapsed if Germany had won the First World War.

The establishment of Weimar and its constitution

Revised

A new system

Following elections in January 1919, a National Assembly met in the city of Weimar to agree a new constitution. The largest party in the Assembly was the SPD which had won 38 per cent of the vote. SPD representatives wished to create a democracy that secured rights for workers, but they had to co-operate with the other pro-democracy parties such as the Centre Party and the **DDP**.

The Weimar Republic

This is the name often given to Germany between 1919 and 1933. It refers to a period of democracy in Germany and takes its name from the city where the new constitution was agreed.

The constitution

- A president was to be elected every seven years with the power to select and dismiss the chancellor. The chancellor formed the government.
- The president was supreme commander of the armed forces.
- The president could **dissolve** the lower house of the German parliament, the Reichstag, and call new Reichstag elections.
- The chancellor and government were accountable to the Reichstag and had to resign if they lost the confidence of the Reichstag.
- The Reichstag was to be elected every four years. There was **universal suffrage** for people over the age of 20.
- **Proportional representation** would be used to conduct elections.
- Germany was a **federal** state: it was divided into eighteen states each of which had their own parliament and local powers. The state parliaments sent representatives to the **Reichsrat**, part of the German parliament. The Reichsrat could propose amendments or delay legislation passed by the Reichstag.
- A **referendum** on single issues could be held if enough people petitioned for one.

The Bill of Rights

The Weimar Republic's constitution also included certain rights:

- **Freedom of association**, speech and religion.
- The right to work: the government should ensure that everyone had a job or, failing that, provide financial assistance.
- The right to own property was guaranteed.

Emergency provisions

Under Article 48 of the constitution, the president had the power to rule via presidential **decree** in the event of an emergency, although this power was kept in check, as the Reichstag could review and overturn any decree issued under Article 48.

Positive features of the Weimar Republic's constitution

The constitution was very democratic with an elected head of state (the president) and a parliament elected by universal suffrage under a proportional representation system. The constitution also contained **checks and balances** to attempt to ensure that no one part of the political system could become too powerful. The constitution also protected many basic **civil rights**.

Criticisms of the Weimar Republic's constitution

The constitution has been criticised for giving too much power to the president under Article 48. Proportional representation has been condemned for creating a fragmented party system and making it difficult to form durable coalition governments. Then again, perhaps it was not the constitution that was flawed: the Weimar Republic faced enormous challenges regardless of the constitutional arrangements.

Spot the mistake

a

Below are a sample exam-style question and a paragraph written in answer to this question. Why does this paragraph not get into Level 4? Once you have identified the mistake, rewrite the paragraph so that it displays the qualities of Level 4. The mark scheme on page 68 will help you.

The Weimar constitution was the prime cause of the instability of the German government between 1919 and 1933. How far do you agree with this view?

To some extent, the constitution of the Weimar Republic was responsible for political instability in Germany between 1919 and 1933. Weimar's constitution led to weak governments and helped extremists. In this way, the constitution caused political instability.

Support or challenge?

Below is a sample exam-style question which asks how far you agree with a specific statement. Below this is a series of general statements which are relevant to the question. Using your own knowledge and the information on the opposite page, decide whether these statements support or challenge the statement given in the question and tick the appropriate box.

'The constitution of the Weimar Republic was responsible for political instability in Germany in the years 1919–1933'. How far do you agree with this statement?

	SUPPORT	CHALLENGE
The president of the Weimar Republic was elected every seven years.		
The constitution had many checks and balances.		
The president could dissolve the Reichstag.		
The electoral system was proportional representation.		
Many of governments in Weimar were short-lived.		
Referenda could be held on single issues.		
The constitution of Weimar was a very democratic one.		

Weimar's problems 1919–1923: the legacy of war

Revised

Weimar Germany had been born of revolution, defeat and social and economic turmoil and in its early years the Republic struggled to overcome various political and economic challenges.

The legacy of war

Defeat in the First World War created a number of problems for the new democracy.

- Democratic politicians had no real option but to sign the armistice which ended war in November 1918. Many Germans then unfairly blamed these politicians for the defeat and labelled them the 'November Criminals'.
- The 'stab in the back myth', which falsely portrayed the revolution and betrayal by democratic and **left-wing** politicians for Germany's defeat (see page 6), was widely believed in some sections of German society and served to undermine support for Weimar Germany.
- Disillusionment with the new Republic set in when the Treaty of Versailles was signed, as this imposed harsh conditions on Germany despite the formation of the new democracy.
- An additional negative legacy of the war was that its cost produced inflation (see page 6) which contributed to post-war economic problems.

The Treaty of Versailles

The Treaty of Versailles was the peace treaty between Germany and her opponents in the First World War. As part of the Treaty:

- Germany's army was restricted to 100,000 men. The navy was reduced to only six battleships with no submarines. An air force was not permitted
- Germany lost territory, including its overseas colonies. Germany also lost West Posen and West Prussia to newly created Poland, and Alsace and Lorraine to France
- the Rhineland, which bordered France, was **demilitarised** and the Saarland placed under **League of Nations** control
- union with Austria, ***Anschluss***, was banned. Germany had to accept liability for the war in the 'war guilt' clause and pay reparations (eventually set at £6600 million in 1921) to the victors for damages incurred during the war.

The Treaty was widely reviled in Germany as a '*diktat*', or dictated peace.

Lack of public support for democracy

Another problem Weimar faced was that the majority of Germans did not wholeheartedly support the new democratic system. The first election in 1919 produced a majority for the pro-Weimar parties but the 1920 election saw their support slump to only 45 per cent.

The persistence of the old regime

A further issue was that much of the old elite of the Second Reich remained in place as the SPD, seeking to promote stability and avoid the possibility of army rebellion, reached a compromise with the army in the Ebert–Groener Pact. This deal left the armed forces, judiciary and civil service unreformed and still containing Second Reich personnel. These elements from the old regime sometimes undermined democracy. In 1920, the army did not support the government during the **Kapp Putsch** (see page 12), and the judiciary's response to the right-wing rebellions was weak. Hitler, found guilty of treason in 1924 after the **Munich Putsch** (see page 26), was sentenced to only five years in jail and served just nine months. The lack of support from some of the elite undermined the new system.

Simple essay style

Below is a sample exam-style question. Use your own knowledge and the information on the opposite page to produce a plan for this question. Choose four general points and provide three pieces of specific information to support each general point. Once you have planned your essay, write the introduction and conclusion for the essay. The introduction should list the points to be discussed in the essay. The conclusion should summarise the key points and justify which point was the most important.

How far was the Treaty of Versailles responsible for the instability of the Weimar Republic in the years 1919–1923?

Develop the detail

Below are a sample exam-style question and a paragraph written in answer to this question. The paragraph contains a limited amount of detail. Annotate the paragraph to add additional detail to the answer.

How accurate is it to say that the Treaty of Versailles was mainly responsible for the political and economic instability in Germany in the years 1919–1923?

It is not accurate to say that the Treaty of Versailles was mainly responsible for the political and economic instability in Germany in the years 1919–1923. The Treaty of Versailles did contribute, however, to political and economic instability in the country at this time. The Treaty contained many aspects that people in Germany did not like and this helped extremists in Germany to gain support: Germans regarded the Treaty as a diktat. Dislike of the Treaty of Versailles reduced many people's support for the Weimar system. In addition, the payment of reparations that the Treaty entailed added to the inflation that Germany had, and this increased economic instability.

Weimar's problems 1919–1923: extremist threats

Revised

Left-wing and right-wing extremists were opposed to democracy in Germany and constituted a major threat to it. Some on the extreme left wished to see Germany become a communist state akin to the **Soviet Union**, whilst those on the extreme right wanted a system more similar to the old regime.

The threat from the extreme left

The Spartacist Uprising, 1919

In 1919, the Spartacists (see page 4) took advantage of a large political protest in Berlin to launch an attempted communist revolution. President Ebert ordered the paramilitary ***Freikorps*** to crush it. The leaders of the Spartacists, Rosa Luxembourg and Karl Liebknecht, were killed.

Strikes, risings and communist takeover

Widespread strike action and communist street violence contributed to the atmosphere of instability in Germany in the early 1920s. Communists also temporarily took control or rebelled in a number of areas: Bavaria in 1919, the Ruhr in 1920 and Saxony and Thuringia in 1923. With Ebert's support, the army and sometimes the *Freikorps* acted to crush these rebellions.

Fear of communism

The activities of left-wing revolutionaries and the success of the communist takeover in Russia caused many to fear communist revolution in Germany. This fear led some to overlook the threat posed by the extreme right, who in reality were probably the greater danger.

The threat from the extreme right

The Kapp Putsch 1920

Following an attempt to disband part of the *Freikorps*, a group of right-wing politicians and soldiers who opposed this move seized control of government in Berlin. Ebert and his ministers fled to Stuttgart. This attempted putsch was named after one of its leaders, Wolfgang Kapp. It lacked the support of both the general public (in Berlin a huge general strike against the putsch was staged) and many of the elite, and so collapsed. Another example of a right-wing attempt to overthrow Weimar was the Munich Putsch in 1923 (see page 26).

The elite

The elite were a group of people in Germany who were the most powerful because of their wealth, social status or political power. They included business leaders and those at the top of the army, judiciary and civil service. Many had a conservative outlook and were not strong supporters of democracy.

Assassinations and violence

Anti-Weimar paramilitary groups carried out political attacks on their opponents between 1919 and 1922 and created a destabilising atmosphere of violence on the streets. Right-wing **death squads**, primarily the group Organisation Consul, carried out 354 political assassinations. These included the murder of prominent politicians such as former finance minister and Centre Party member Matthias Erzberger in 1921, and foreign minister and industrialist Walther Rathenau in 1922.

Political assassinations

- Between January 1919 and June 1922 there were a total of 376 political murders in Germany.
- Of the 354 murders committed by sympathisers of the right, 326 went unpunished. Just one life sentence and a total of 90 years in prison were handed out.
- Of the 22 murders committed by sympathisers of the left, four went unpunished. Ten death sentences, three life sentences and a total of 250 years in prison were handed out.

Ideas

The nationalist right did not just undermine Weimar through direct action. Ideas such as the 'stab in the back' myth made democracy appear weak and un-German, and portrayed democratic politicians as traitors.

Mind map

Use the information on the opposite page to add detail to the mind map below.

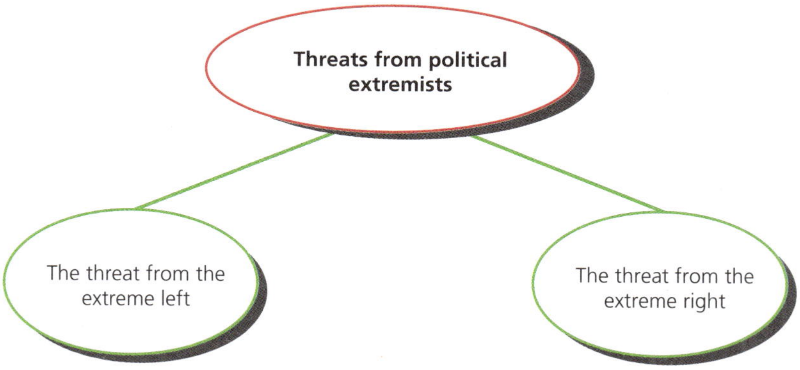

Spectrum of significance

Below are a sample exam-style question and a list of general points which could be used to answer the question. Use your own knowledge and the information on the opposite page to reach a judgement about the importance of these general points to the question posed. Write numbers on the spectrum below to indicate their relative importance. Having done this, write a brief justification of your placement, explaining why some of these factors are more important than others. The resulting diagram could form the basis of an essay plan.

How far do you agree that the threat from the extreme right was a more significant challenge to the stability of the Weimar Republic than the threat from the extreme left?

1. The extreme right promoted ideas, such as the 'stab in the back' myth, which undermined support for the Weimar Republic.
2. The extreme right were responsible for many political murders and much political violence.
3. The extreme right were responsible for a number of attempts to overthrow the government.
4. The extreme left were behind a number of risings and large-scale strikes.
5. Many people in Weimar feared that the extreme left would cause a communist revolution.

More significant ⟷ Less significant

Revised

Weimar's problems 1919–1923: 1923, the crisis year

In 1923, many of the political and economic problems of Weimar Germany reached crisis point as inflation spiralled out of control, the Ruhr was invaded and the Nazis attempted to overthrow the government.

The inflationary problem

Wartime and demobilisation inflation

- The First World War left Germany with high inflation. Much of the cost of the war had been financed by increasing the supply of money and the German currency consequently declined in value.
- Wartime shortages exacerbated the problem and caused price rises.
- In the aftermath of the war, government expenditure remained high as the government had to support war widows, injured war veterans and demobilised soldiers.
- Furthermore, the new constitution made social security a constitutional right, which obligated the government to support the unemployed.

Reparations

From 1921, the inflationary problem increased when reparations payments commenced.

- One difficulty Germany faced in meeting its reparations obligations was that most of the reparations had to be paid for in **gold marks**, which held their value as the currency declined.
- As inflation increased and the value of the German currency weakened, paying for reparations became an ever more expensive burden.
- In 1922, the German government sought to suspend their reparations payments but were refused permission.
- By early 1923, Germany was failing to meet all of its reparations obligations.

The Ruhr crisis

In January 1923 the French and Belgian governments responded to German failure to pay all reparations by ordering the invasion of the German industrial region, the Ruhr. Their armies occupied factories and mines, and seized raw materials and goods in lieu of reparations. With government support, workers and business owners in the Ruhr followed a policy of **passive resistance**, refusing to co-operate with the occupying forces by going on strike. The German government paid the workers and compensated owners for lost revenue, thus adding to government expenditure. The situation in the Ruhr further damaged the German economy.

Hyperinflation

The already profound problem of inflation in Germany ran out of control in the aftermath of the Ruhr crisis as confidence in the German currency collapsed: the mark now became worthless. To try to meet spending obligations, the government printed more and more money, which added to the problem. In 1923, 300 paper mills and 150 printing presses worked 24 hours a day to print money. While the new government of Gustav Stresemann struggled to resolve the situation, the Nazis, an extremist right-wing political party formed in 1919, launched a failed putsch in Munich in November 1923. In the end the issue of hyperinflation was resolved (see page 16) but not without causing a great shock to Germans, many of whom saw their savings eradicated or standard of living dramatically reduced. However, debtors, including many large business owners, benefited as the value of their debts were wiped out by hyperinflation.

▼ Inflation in Germany 1919–1923. The table shows the marks needed to buy one US dollar.

April 1919	Nov 1921	August 1922	January 1923	Sept 1923	Dec 1923
12	263	1000	17,000	98,860,000	4,200,000,000,000 (i.e. 4.2 trillion)

Simple essay style

Below is a sample exam-style question. Use your own knowledge and the information on the opposite page to produce a plan for this question. Choose four general points and provide three pieces of specific information to support each general point. Once you have planned your essay, write the introduction and conclusion for the essay. The introduction should list the points to be discussed in the essay. The conclusion should summarise the key points and justify which point was the most important.

To what extent were the main problems facing Germany in 1923 economic?

Turning assertion into argument

Below are a sample exam-style question and a series of assertions. Read the exam-style question and then add a justification to each of the assertions to turn it into an argument.

How far do you agree that the most significant challenge to the stability of the Weimar Republic in the years 1919–1923 was the threat from political extremists?

Political extremists were a major threat to the stability of the Weimar Republic because

___

___

The legacy of the First World War was also a threat to the stability of the Weimar Republic in the sense that

___

___

Economic problems such as inflation were also a threat to the stability of the Weimar Republic in that

___

___

How did the Weimar Republic survive its early problems?

Revised

Despite political violence, attempted revolution, financial crisis and invasion, Weimar did survive its early period. The weakness of some of Weimar's opponents and the actions of some of its politicians helped Weimar to survive.

The weakness of Weimar's opponents

Weimar's opponents were disunited and often had different political goals. Additionally, they lacked effective organisation and widespread support.

Poor leadership and planning of attempted putsches

The Spartacists did not carefully plan their attempted takeover of power but opportunistically tried to turn a protest into a revolution. During the Munich Putsch, Hitler exhibited indecision as he dithered overnight about whether to launch his **coup**, which gave time to others to alert the authorities. The rebels also marched down a fairly narrow street during the putsch, allowing the Bavarian police to trap the rebels and defeat them.

Lack of support from the public

Many Germans were ambivalent about the Republic yet there was not widespread support for extremists. The Spartacists had only around 15,000 members and a huge general strike brought down the government established by Kapp. There was a considerable degree of popular opposition to extremism. For example, following the murder of Walther Rathenau in 1922 (see page 12), 700,000 people demonstrated in Berlin against political violence.

The actions of Ebert and Stresemann

President Ebert

Ebert acted ruthlessly against the Spartacists and other left-wing rebels such as those in the Ruhr in 1920. He also led the call for a general strike in Berlin during the Kapp Putsch (see page 12). Ebert ruled under Article 48 briefly during the Munich Putsch which enabled him to take control of the situation.

Gustav Stresemann

As chancellor, Stresemann helped to solve the Ruhr crisis of 1923 by calling off passive resistance to French occupation. This reduced government payments and calmed the situation. Stresemann recognised that international confidence in Germany would only be restored if Germany met its obligations and so he restarted reparations payments. To pay for this, government spending was cut (700,000 state employees were sacked) and Stresemann worked to negotiate the Dawes Plan. This alleviated the burden of reparations payments and provided US loans and investment to assist the German economy. In addition, Stresemann worked with banker Hjalmar Schacht and finance minister Hans Luther to resolve inflation. The old currency was abolished and a new currency, the **Rentenmark**, was established. One unit of the new currency was worth one trillion of the old. **Collateral** for the new currency was provided by linking the new currency to German industrial and agricultural assets.

> **The Dawes Plan 1924**
>
> Banker Charles Dawes led an international committee which redesigned reparations. The annual payment of gold marks was reduced to 1 million between 1924 and 1929. An international loan was made available to help Germany pay.

Other factors helping Weimar Germany's survival

- The elite: Despite the ambivalence of many in the elite for the new political system, some members of the elite helped it to survive. The army enthusiastically crushed left-wing rebellions and supported the government during the Munich Putsch. The civil service and banking community refused to co-operate with the Kapp government.
- Support from the international community: The Dawes Plan of 1924 helped to stabilise the German economy and currency.

Developing an argument

Below is a sample exam-style question, a list of key points to be made in the essay, and a paragraph from the essay. Read the question, the plan, and the sample paragraph. Rewrite the paragraph in order to develop an argument. Your paragraph should explain why the factor discussed is either the most significant factor or less significant than the other factor.

How far did the Weimar Republic survive its early problems because of the mistakes of its opponents?

Key points

- The mistakes of Weimar's opponents.
- Lack of support for extremists.
- The actions of Ebert and Stresemann.
- The Dawes Plan 1924.

Sample paragraph

Weimar's opponents, such as the extreme left and extreme right, did not succeed in their aim of overthrowing the Republic partially because of their mistakes. For example, the Spartacists did not plan their attempted takeover of power in 1919 well, and Hitler was indecisive at the start of the Munich Putsch in 1923, and also did not have a very good route planned for his rebels to march. These mistakes by political extremists who opposed Weimar helped the Republic to survive.

You're the examiner

a

Below are a sample exam-style question and an opening paragraph written in answer to this question. Read the paragraph and the mark scheme provided on page 68. Decide which level you would award the paragraph. Write a level below, along with a justification for your decision.

To what extent were the weaknesses of the opponents of the Weimar Republic responsible for its survival between 1919 and 1923?

To an extent the weaknesses of the opponents of the Weimar Republic account for its survival. One weakness of the political extremists who wished to destroy the Weimar Republic was that they lacked sufficient public support. The Spartacists, who launched a failed attempt to create a communist revolution in 1919, were a small group with only 15,000 members, for example. Similarly, during the Munich Putsch the Nazi Party did not succeed in generating widespread support for their cause. Furthermore, active public opposition to the actions of political extremists can be seen on a number of occasions, such as in 1920 when a huge general strike was a significant factor in the defeat of the Kapp Putsch, and in 1922 when 700,000 people in Berlin demonstrated their opposition to political murders following the murder of foreign minister Rathenau. Political assassinations by the extreme right ended after this demonstration. The lack of sufficient support for the political extremists helped the Weimar Republic to survive: extremists did not have the strength to overthrow the Republic and at times their actions were opposed by the public, which helped Weimar to continue.

Level: Reason for choosing this level:

The golden era 1924–1929: politics and economics

Revised

The years 1924–1929 saw economic improvements and greater political stability in Germany. During this era, sometimes referred to as the 'golden' years, support for democracy increased, the economy grew and Germany gained acceptance in the international community. However, underneath the apparently stable and successful surface, Germany still had a great many problems.

Were the golden years really so golden? Politics and economics

	Positive features	Negative features
Politics	Increased political stability: • No putsch attempts. • No political assassinations. • The creation of the Grand Coalition in 1928: this coalition, led by Hermann Müller of the SPD, was a coalition of the left, right and centre and commanded a secure majority (over 60%) in the Reichstag. Increased acceptance of democracy: • By the 1928 election 76% of people supported pro-Weimar parties. • Support for the Nazis was very low: they obtained only 2.6% of the vote in 1928. The role of Hindenburg: • Despite his authoritarian past, President Hindenburg upheld the new constitution and, in 1928, chose a SPD Chancellor, despite his hostility to socialism.	Immature party politics and unstable coalitions: • Political parties, which were unused to the real political power that the new constitution gave them, did not work together well. The SPD were often reluctant to co-operate with others while governments were sometimes brought down by trivial issues, such as the collapse of Luther's 1926 administration over the issue of what the German flag should look like. • Forming stable coalition governments proved difficult. There were seven governments between 1923 and 1929. Some governments did not have a majority in the Reichstag. Support for extremists: • Support for extremists had reduced but it remained worryingly high with a quarter of people voting for parties that wished to see Weimar democracy end: the **KPD**, German Communist Party, obtained 10.6% of the vote in 1928. The role of Hindenburg: • Hindenburg was obstructive to the idea of working with the SPD before 1928 and also had, until that time, insisted that the far right **DNVP** be included in coalitions.
Economics	Economic growth and development: • By 1928, production equalled that of 1913 and national income was 12% higher than in 1913. • Certain sectors of the economy performed particularly well: chemicals company I.G. Farben became the largest manufacturer in Europe. • Exports rose by 40% between 1925 and 1929. • Loans from the international community, particularly the USA, financed the development of infrastructure in Germany: 25.5 billion marks were loaned between 1924 and 1930. • Inflation remained relatively low. • Unemployment ran at a relatively low level. Improved standards of living: • Wages rose every year between 1924 and 1929.	A sluggish agricultural sector: • Agriculture was in recession from 1927. Dependence on the USA: • When the effects of the Wall Street Crash and the **Great Depression** started to hit Germany, credit dried up and the USA sought repayment of loans. Problematic unemployment: • Unemployment did not fall below 1.3 million and levels were climbing before 1929. Economic weaknesses: • The German economy did not perform as well as comparable economies, such as Britain and France. Social tensions: • Tensions remained high between workers and business owners: industrial disputes were common.

Support or challenge?

Below is a sample exam-style question which asks how far you agree with a specific statement. Below this are a series of general statements which are relevant to the question. Using your own knowledge and the information on the opposite page decide whether these statements support or challenge the statement in the question and tick the appropriate box.

'The Weimar Republic was strong and stable in the years 1924–1929'. How far do you agree with this statement?

	SUPPORT	CHALLENGE
The Grand Coalition commanded a secure majority in the Reichstag in 1928.		
There was economic growth in Germany 1924–1929.		
The German economy was very dependent upon American money.		
Agriculture was in recession from 1927.		
There were seven governments between 1923 and 1929.		
In the 1928 election 76 per cent of people supported pro-Weimar parties.		
The KPD obtained 10.6 per cent of the vote in 1929.		
Wages rose every year between 1924 and 1929.		

Introducing an argument

Below are a sample exam-style question, a list of key points to be made in the essay, and a simple introduction and conclusion for the essay. Read the question, the plan, and the introduction and conclusion. Rewrite the introduction and the conclusion to develop an argument.

How far do you agree that by 1929 the Weimar Republic had resolved its political and economic problems?

Key points

- Political improvements.
- Economic improvements.
- Remaining political problems.
- Remaining economic problems.

Introduction

By 1929, the political and economic problems of the Weimar Republic had been partially resolved. There were political and economic improvements, but also still some political and economic problems.

Conclusion

The Weimar Republic's political and economic problems were partially solved by 1929. For example, there were political improvements, but also some remaining problems.

The golden era 1924–1929: foreign policy and culture

Revised

Foreign policy

There were many positive developments in the arena of foreign policy 1924–1929 as Germany was reconciled with the international community. The politician most associated with these policies was Gustav Stresemann, a member of the **DVP** party, who had originally opposed the Weimar Republic, but became one of its strongest defenders. Stresemann was chancellor in 1923 and foreign minister 1923–1929.

- The end of the Ruhr crisis: Stresemann's actions had ended the Ruhr crisis. France and Belgium left the Ruhr in 1925.
- Reparations: as foreign minister, Stresemann pursued a policy of fulfilment of Germany's international obligations through payments of reparations. Fulfilment enabled Stresemann to renegotiate reparations and gain foreign loans and investment through the Dawes Plan of 1924 and the Young Plan of 1929.
- Borders: In 1925, as part of the Locarno Pact, Stresemann agreed to Germany's post war borders with France.
- League of Nations: Germany was admitted to the League of Nations in 1926.

All of this created a climate of optimism in Europe about the prospects for future peace. However, the nationalist right were opposed to the acceptance of the Treaty of Versailles that German involvement in the international community implied.

The Young Plan, 1929

An international agreement easing the burden of reparations on Germany, the Young Plan increased the repayment term to 59 years and reduced annual repayments. The Young Plan was opposed by the nationalist right. A right-wing coalition, including the DNVP and the Nazis with some backing from nationalist industrialists such as the steel magnate Fritz Thyssen, organised a referendum opposing the Young Plan. Their motion only attracted the support of 13.9% of people who voted.

Weimar culture and society in the 1920s

Newly democratic Germany saw a flourishing of cultural experimentation and a more liberal and tolerant atmosphere. Society also reflected these values: gay culture flourished in Berlin, and some young women in cities were able to pursue careers and live in an independent manner. Many Germans did not regard these cultural changes positively, however, and came to associate the Weimar system with **decadence** and experimentation. Outside of large urban areas, most Germans still preferred traditional culture, traditional roles for women and did not tolerate homosexuality.

Weimar artistic culture

- In art, George Grosz and Otto Dix produced works reflecting on the impact of the First World War and satirising the **Junker class.**
- In architecture and design the hugely influential **Bauhaus** movement created modern designs for buildings, furniture and graphics.
- In music, American jazz became very popular and began to influence the sound of German popular music. There was a lively jazz scene in Berlin.
- In literature, Erich Maria Remarque's *All Quiet On the Western Front* (1929) looked at the traumatic impact of the First World War on German soldiers.
- In cinema, Germany had a world-leading industry. **Expressionist** works, such as Fritz Lang's *Metropolis* (1927), were particularly influential.
- Satirical forms of **cabaret** were popular in Berlin.

Identify an argument

Below are a series of definitions, a sample exam-style question and two sample conclusions. One of the conclusions achieves a high level because it contains an argument. The other achieves a lower level because it contains only description and assertion. Identify which is which. The mark scheme on page 68 will help you.

- **Description:** a detailed account.
- **Assertion:** a statement of fact or an opinion, which is not support by a reason.
- **Reason:** a statement which explains or justifies something.
- **Argument:** an assertion justified with a reason.

How accurate is it to say that German foreign policy was responsible for the political instability of the Weimar Republic in the years 1924–1929?

Sample 1

To some extent the political stability of the Weimar Republic 1924–1929 was determined by its foreign policy. The Young Plan was an international agreement that reduced the level of reparations and also increased the amount of time that Germany had to pay them. The Dawes Plan was a similar scheme in 1924. Furthermore, Stresemann agreed Germany's western borders in the Locarno Pact, and Germany joined the League of Nations in 1926.

Sample 2

To some extent the political stability of the Weimar Republic 1924–1929 was determined by its foreign policy. The Dawes Plan of 1924 and the Young Plan of 1929 assisted with economic stability by reducing the burden of reparations and arranging for foreign loans which helped to grow the German economy. Furthermore, political stability was improved as Stresemann improved relations with France. The Locarno Pact of 1925, for example, saw Germany agree to its borders with France. This reduced tensions and made destabilising events, such as the occupation of the Ruhr, less likely.

Recommended reading

Below is a list of suggested further reading on this topic.

- *Weimar Germany: Promise and Tragedy*, pages 7–41, Eric D. Weitz (2007)
- *The Weimar Republic,* pages 50–57, Stephen J. Lee (1998)
- *Weimar Germany, The Republic of the Reasonable*, pages 145–59, Paul Bookbinder (1997)

Revised

Exam focus

Below is a sample A-grade essay. Read it and the examiner comments around it.

How far were political extremists the main threat to the stability of the Weimar Republic in the years 1919–1929?

> This is a focused introduction that outlines the structure of the rest of the essay.

Political extremists caused a major challenge to the stability of the Weimar Republic through actions such as the Spartacist Uprising and the Kapp Putsch. However, an equally important threat to Weimar's stability was the economic problems that the Republic faced. In addition the legacy of the First World War and certain features of Weimar's constitution contributed to the instability that the Republic experienced during 1919–1929.

> The paragraph gives a detailed analysis of the first years of the Weimar Republic. The use of dates shows an excellent grasp of the period.

Political extremists undermined the stability of the Weimar Republic in a number of ways. They threatened the existence of the Republic by seeking to overthrow it on a number of occasions. In 1919, for example, the Spartacists, a communist political group, sought to turn a demonstration in Berlin into a communist revolution, while in 1920, a group of right-wing nationalists and supporters of the Freikorps temporarily seized control of the government in Berlin. The Nazi Party also sought to seize power in 1923. These attempted 'putsches' were serious, but none succeeded. In some respects a more damaging impact that political extremists had was in the more routine violence that they committed. The extreme right was particularly responsible for this and carried out 354 political murders, including senior politicians such as Erzberger in 1921 and Rathenau in 1922. The SA, the armed wing of the Nazi Party, also committed many violent attacks on their political opponents. Furthermore, the extreme left destabilised the Republic through strikes and uprisings such as those in the Ruhr in 1920. Political extremists, by use of violence and attempts to rebel, created a climate of fear, and therefore posed a major threat to the stability of the Weimar Republic.

> The second sentence of the paragraph analyses the importance of the 'stab in the back' myth, by explaining how it weakened the Republic.

Furthermore, the ideas of political extremists undermined the stability of the Weimar Republic. The 'stab in the back' myth, promoted by the extreme right, suggested that democratic politicians, Jews and socialists had caused Germany's defeat in the First World War. This myth weakened support for the Weimar Republic and democracy. In addition, communist ideas damaged support for democracy and created a fear of revolution that led some to embrace the anti-democratic extreme right. Overall, the actions and ideas of political extremists damaged the stability of the Weimar Republic because they weakened the Republic.

> This paragraph broadens the range of factors the essay considers by focusing on economics.

However, perhaps even more damaging to Weimar were the economic problems that the Republic faced. The cost of fighting in the First World War was financed to a significant extent by printing money, and this, along with the shortages that the war caused, led to inflation. The burden of the post-war costs of demobilisation and the need from 1921 to pay reparations led to further inflation as the German government desperately printed money to try to keep up with its payments. This inflationary crisis culminated in the single largest crisis for Weimar during 1919–1923, when the French and Belgium armies invaded the Ruhr after Germany stopped paying reparations. This caused inflation to run out of control: at its worst, in 1923, 4.2 trillion marks were needed to buy one US dollar. The financial and inflationary crisis caused a major threat to the stability of the Weimar Republic as it led to the invasion of the Ruhr by foreign powers, money becoming worthless, declining living standards and savings being wiped out. The inflationary crisis represented a huge threat to the stability of Weimar because it indicated that the Republic was failing and therefore many people began to support extremists.

Additionally, underlying many of the challenges that Weimar faced was the legacy of the First World War. The costs of the war that were a major factor in causing inflation, and the reparations that resulted from losing the war, added to this problem. The strain of fighting the war and the legacy of defeat in the war contributed significantly to the creation of political extremism and the damaging 'stab in the back' myth. Clearly, the legacy of the war was a threat to the stability of the Weimar Republic because it caused long-term problems that democratic governments found hard to solve.

Finally, the constitution of Weimar contributed to instability in a limited way, as the use of a proportional representation system made it difficult to form stable governments. Between 1923 and 1929 there were seven coalition governments in Weimar Germany. In this way the constitution was a threat to the stability of the Republic as it was difficult to form strong governments.

In conclusion, political extremists posed a major threat to the stability of the Weimar Republic through their attempts to overthrow the system and through their use of violence and their damaging ideas. However, at least as much of a problem for Weimar was the hugely destabilising effect of the Ruhr crisis and hyperinflation. Furthermore, underlying many of these destabilising factors was the impact of the First World War. Overall, political extremists were a major but not the only or necessarily the main challenge to the stability of the Weimar Republic.

The paragraph raises the level of detail in the essay by using precise statistics.

This paragraph deals with a factor that affected the Republic's stability right up until 1929. Together with earlier paragraphs, it means the essay deals with the whole of the period specified in the question.

The conclusion rounds off the argument by examining how political extremism relates to the other factors mentioned in the essay.

26/30

This is a sustained response which would obtain a mark low in Level 5. The candidate explores the factor given in the question in detail, but also looks at the significance of a number of other factors. Accurate detail supports the argument, and the question is focused throughout. The essay does not get full marks as it is primarily focused on the period 1919–1923 and therefore lacks balance.

Reverse engineering

The best essays are based on careful plans. Read the essay and the examiner's comment and try to work out the general points of the plan used to write the essay. Once you have done this, note down the specific examples used to support each point.

Section 2:
The rise of the Third Reich

The ideas and origins of the Nazi Party

Revised

Hitler did not overthrow the Weimar Republic, but was appointed chancellor in January 1933. The factors that enabled this to happen are complex. To understand the circumstances of Hitler's and the Nazis' rise to power it is important to examine the ideas and origins of the party.

Origins

The **DAP (German Workers' Party)** was founded by Anton Drexler in politically unstable Munich in the aftermath of the First World War. Despite the party's socialist-sounding name, Drexler hoped to attract German workers away from support for socialism and communism and towards support for a nationalist agenda by addressing their concerns.

The German army sent Adolf Hitler, an Austrian national who had served in the German army during the First World War, to report upon the DAP's activities. At this time the party was very small and had very little impact but, interested in the DAP's stance, Hitler joined and soon made an impact through his powerful **oratory**. His speeches condemned the Treaty of Versailles and communists, and blamed Jews for Germany's problems. The party was now renamed the National Socialist German Workers' Party (or NSDAP, commonly referred to as the Nazis). In 1920, Drexler and Hitler drew up the party programme, the 25 Points, and in 1921 Hitler became leader, or *Führer*, of the Party.

Ideas

The 25 Points contained the key elements of the Nazi Party message. Hitler developed this ideology in speeches and his books, *Mein Kampf* (1925) and *Zweites Buch* (1928).

His main ideas were:

- German nationalism: Germany should be strong, and all German-speaking peoples should be united to help maximise German strength. To develop German power, colonial expansion into eastern Europe was needed. This 'living space' was called ***lebensraum***. The Treaty of Versailles should be overturned.
- Racial ideas: at the core of Hitler's ideas were false notions about race. These ideas had their origins in the pseudo-scientific notions of the day. Hitler believed there were profound and significant differences between racial groups. Furthermore, he thought that races were organised into a hierarchy with **Aryans**, a Germanic-Nordic race, at the top. In his view, racial purity equalled national strength.
- **Anti-Semitism**: Hitler believed Jews were an inferior race and that Aryan strength would be compromised and polluted through interbreeding with Jews. Hitler also believed that Jews were engaged in a plot to sap Aryan racial strength through interbreeding.
- Social Darwinism: Hitler also subscribed to Social Darwinist ideas. Hitler used the notion of the 'survival of the fittest' as a moral principle. He believed that not only did the fittest or strongest of species survive, but also that it was morally right for the strongest to triumph. Thus 'weaker' races should be eradicated.

Fascism

The philosophy of Hitler and the Nazis was fascism. Fascism combines a usually racist nationalism with militarism and belief in a strong state and strong authoritarian leadership. Fascism is anti-democratic and anti-socialist.

Spot the mistake

Below are a sample exam-style question and a paragraph written in answer to this question. Why does the paragraph not get into Level 4? Once you have identified the mistake, rewrite the paragraph so that it displays the qualities of Level 4. The mark scheme on page 68 will help you.

How far was Nazi ideology the main reason for the increase in support for the Nazi Party 1928–1932?

Nazi ideology appealed to some people in Germany. Nazi ideas included extreme German nationalism and anti-Semitism. Hitler also said that he hated the Treaty of Versailles and communists. After the First World War, Germany was forced to sign the Treaty of Versailles.

Mind map

Use the information on the opposite page to add detail to the mind map below.

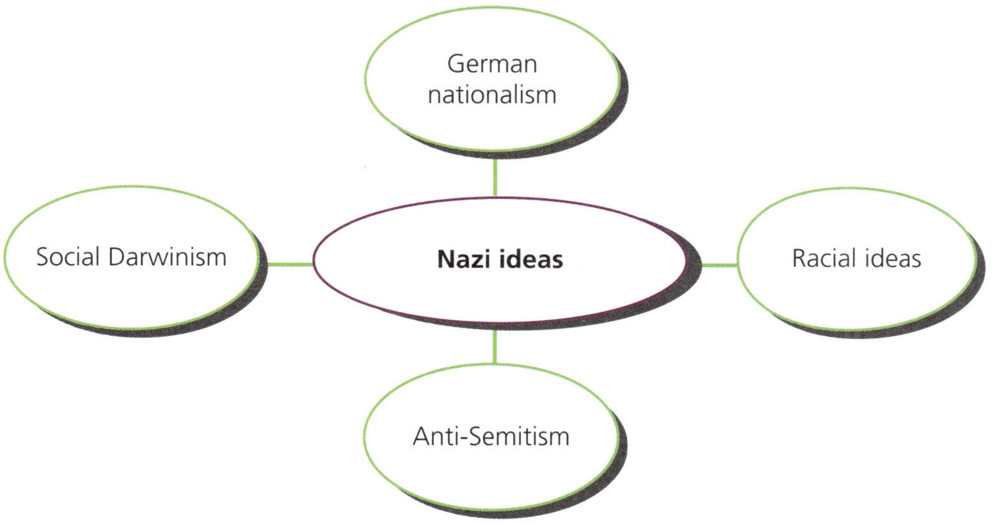

The early years of the Nazi Party

Revised

The Munich Putsch, November 1923

In the early 1920s, Hitler cultivated links with the elite in Munich and started to build up support for the party. He also worked with Ernst Röhm to develop an armed wing, the ***Sturmabteilung* (SA)**. In the atmosphere of crisis in Germany, in late 1923 (see page 14), Hitler launched an attempted takeover of government. On 8 November in a beer hall in Munich, Hitler and Röhm, with the backing of ex-military leader General Ludendorff, took control of a **conservative** political meeting. Hitler announced a national revolution and hoped to unite right-wing nationalists in an armed march to seize control. Some of the conservative politicians, upon whose support Hitler had counted, instead reported the plot to the authorities. Bavarian police were able to stop the **putsch** as its participants marched through Munich on 9 November.

Wilderness years

Following the putsch, Hitler and other conspirators were put on trial. Despite the judge's evident sympathy for the Nazis' cause, Hitler was found guilty of treason. However, he only received a short sentence. After the putsch, the Nazis were banned in Bavaria. With Hitler in jail and the now illegal party led by the ineffectual Alfred Rosenberg, the Nazis were weak and in disarray. The putsch did produce several benefits for Hitler, however:

- Hitler's imprisonment gave him the time to write his political book, *Mein Kampf*, or 'My Struggle'. Sales of *Mein Kampf* helped support Hitler in his political work after his release.
- Hitler reconsidered his tactics following the putsch. He decided to use the Weimar system and try to gain power through electoral success rather than force.

Upon Hitler's release, he set about regaining a grip on the party and reorganising the party machine:

- Hitler persuaded the Chancellor of Bavaria to lift the ban on the party in 1925.
- The ***Schutzstaffel* (SS)**, a small bodyguard for Hitler led by Heinrich Himmler, was formed in 1925.
- At the **Bamberg Conference** in 1926 Hitler asserted his ideology and the ***Führerprinzip***.
- Hitler also established a national party network during this time. Regional party bosses called ***Gauleiter*** were appointed by, and accountable to, Hitler. This party structure assisted with election campaigning and the eventual takeover by the Nazi Party.
- This era also saw the development of many of the Nazi organisations that would later help the Nazis to develop their support amongst various groups in German society. The Hitler Youth was formally established as the Nazi Party's youth movement in 1926, whilst Nazi organisations were set up for doctors and teachers, and an agricultural movement was established in 1930 to try to draw in the peasantry.
- Nazi Party membership grew from 27,000 people in 1925 to 108,000 in 1928.

Despite these efforts and the development of Nazi propaganda under Joseph Goebbels, the Nazi Party made very little impact in the 1928 election, gaining only 2.6 per cent of the vote. The Nazis did see their support increase in some rural areas such as Schleswig-Holstein. This may indicate that where people had experienced economic hardship, as in many rural areas, the Nazi message had some impact.

The *Führerprinzip*

The *Führerprinzip* is the principle that Hitler possessed all power and authority within the Nazi Party. It later became the operating principle for the Nazi state.

Support or challenge?

Below is a sample exam-style question, which asks how far you agree with a specific statement. Below this are a series of general statements which are relevant to the question. Using your own knowledge and the information on the opposite page decide whether these statements support or challenge the statement in the question and tick the appropriate box.

'Developments in the Nazi Party in the 1920s helped the party gain success in elections after 1928.' How far do you agree with this view?

	SUPPORT	CHALLENGE
Hitler established a national Nazi Party network in the 1920s.		
The Nazi Party was banned in Bavaria.		
Alfred Rosenberg was an ineffective leader.		
Hitler wrote *Mein Kampf*.		
Nazi organisations for young people, doctors and teachers were established.		
Hitler was imprisoned.		
Hitler decided to change tactics and try to fight elections.		

Eliminate irrelevance

Below are a sample exam-style question and a paragraph written in answer to this question. Read the paragraph and identify parts of the paragraph that are not directly relevant to the question. Draw a line through the information that is irrelevant and justify your deletions in the margin.

How far do changes to Nazi Party structure and tactics in the 1920s account for their increased popularity after 1928?

The changes that the Nazi Party made in the 1920s account for the Party's increased popularity after 1928 to a limited extent. The improved structure helped the Party in election campaigns. Hitler established a national network of Party organisations headed up by regional Party leaders, the Gauleiter. The local Nazi Party organisations helped to publicise the Party and increase its popularity, and assisted in running election campaigns which helped to increase the Nazis' share of the vote. A number of Nazi organisations were established in the 1920s which later helped draw people into the movement. The Hitler Youth was one of these. After Hitler came to power the Hitler Youth became compulsory and during the Second World War some members even ended up fighting for the Nazis. These measures helped to increase Nazi Party popularity by enabling improved campaigning and by drawing more people into the movement.

Revised

Economic and political crisis 1929–1932

In 1928, the Nazi Party was a small fringe party with minimal support. Yet only four years later it became the most popular political party in Germany, gaining more than 37 per cent of the vote in the July 1932 election. The economic and political crisis that Germany experienced made the Nazis and their message much more appealing.

The economic impact of the Depression

Following the Wall Street **stock market crash** in the United States in October 1929, the American economy experienced a depression as a banking crisis and bankruptcies ensued. The German economy was heavily dependent upon US money and was therefore very exposed when US investment dried up and loans were recalled.

The German economy was severely affected.

- National income shrunk by 39 per cent between 1929 and 1932.
- Industrial production declined by more than 40 per cent.
- The number of unemployed rose to over 6 million (officially) by 1932: one-third of people of working age were out of work.
- 50,000 businesses were bankrupted.
- In 1931, a banking crisis saw the collapse of five major banks.
- Homelessness and poverty increased and people's standard of living decreased. Many felt insecure and desperate.

The political impact of the Depression

The political system struggled to cope with these difficulties and the system of parliamentary government declined:

- The **Grand Coalition** government, led by Müller, fell apart as the parties in government disagreed over the issue of unemployment benefits.
- Following the collapse of the Grand Coalition, subsequent governments were **minority administrations** which lacked **Reichstag** support. Chancellor Brüning's government failed to get backing for its budget in July 1930. Consequently, Hindenburg **dissolved** the Reichstag and called a new election. Chancellor von Papen's government lost a vote of no-confidence in 1932 whilst Chancellor von Schleicher's administration only lasted for two months.

Weimar chancellors 1928–1933	
Hermann Müller	June 1932–March 1930
Heinrich Brüning	March 1930–May 1932
Franz von Papen	May 1932–November 1932
Kurt von Schleicher	December 1932–January 1933

- The German political system moved in a more authoritarian direction in the years before Hitler became chancellor. Brüning and von Papen relied extensively on emergency presidential **decrees** rather than on parliamentary government. For example, there were 44 emergency decrees issued under Article 48 in 1931 compared with just five in 1930. In July 1932, von Papen and Hindenburg also used Article 48 to seize control of regional government in **Prussia**, whose **left-wing SPD** government they objected to.
- Politicians did not take effective action to deal with the Depression. Brüning only started to act in June 1932 by launching modest **reflationary schemes**: he took too little action, too late. German people lost faith in their political system as politicians failed to help them.
- Democratic norms broke down as political violence returned to the streets of Germany. During the July 1932 election campaign there were 461 riots in Prussia in which a number of people died. The SA was responsible for much of the violence as members participated in battles against communists. Street violence added to an air of instability in Germany which served to increase people's discontent.

Spectrum of significance

Below are a sample exam-style question and a list of general points, which could be used to answer the question. Use your own knowledge and the information on the opposite page to reach a judgement about the importance of these general points to the question posed. Write numbers on the spectrum below to indicate their relative importance. Having done this, write a brief justification of your placement, explaining why some of these factors are more important than others. The resulting diagram could form the basis of an essay plan.

How far do you agree that the Nazi Party only increased its popularity during 1928–1932 because Germany was suffering from an economic depression?

1. Hitler's reorganisation of the Nazi Party and change of tactics in the 1920s.
2. The impact of the Depression on Germany.
3. The effectiveness of Nazi propaganda.
4. The popularity of Hitler.
5. The political crisis in Germany 1930–1932.

Depression was not a factor ←→ Depression was the only factor

Turning assertion into argument

Below are a sample exam-style question and a series of assertions. Read the exam-style question and then add a justification to each of the assertions to turn it into an argument.

How far was Hitler only able to come to power because of the political and economic crisis suffered by Germany 1929–1932?

The high level of unemployment in Germany 1930–1932 helped Hitler come to power because

____

____

The failure of Brüning, von Papen and von Schleicher's governments to gain the support of the Reichstag helped Hitler come to power in the sense that

____

____

The failure of politicians to come up with effective solutions to the 1930s Depression helped Hitler to gain power because

____

____

Support for the Nazi Party 1928–1933

Revised

The Depression and political crisis provided an opportunity for the Nazis. As the Depression hit, the Party's electoral success dramatically increased, as did its membership. There were around 2 million members by early 1933. Members were also attracted to Nazi Party organisations such as the Hitler Youth, whose uniforms and hiking appealed to young members. The violent ethos of the SA gave its frequently unemployed members a sense of purpose and an outlet for some of their frustrations.

▼ Nazi party votes in the Reichstag elections.* After these elections, the Nazi Party was the largest in the Reichstag.

Election date	1928	1930	July 1932*
Percentage of the vote	2.6%	18.3%	37.3%
Number of seats	12	107	230

It was the Nazis' popularity in elections and their creation of a mass membership organisation that made Hitler a contender for the chancellorship of Germany.

The demographics of Nazi voters and members

- A much larger number of people voted for the Nazi Party than were members.
- Nazi members were most likely to be young (60% of members in 1930 were aged under 40) and male, partly because the Party did not encourage active female participation.
- However, women were more likely to vote for the Party than men. Hitler had some success in appealing to traditionally minded women who had not voted before.
- Catholics were less likely to support the Nazis than Protestants, as the majority of Catholic voters always supported the Centre Party.
- Urban dwellers were less likely to vote for the Nazis than those who lived in the countryside.
- **Working class** people formed the largest number of Nazi Party members at 31% of members but were, on average, less likely to be members than most other social classes. This apparent paradox can be accounted for because the working class formed the largest social group in Germany, at 46%.
- Office workers and the self-employed or *Mittelstand* were over-represented as Party members.

The impact of propaganda

Nazi propaganda was tailored to different audiences to try to maximise their support.

- Messages about bread and work were deployed in working-class areas.
- Messages about the Weimar Republic's supposedly lax moral standards were tailored to conservative mothers.
- Anti-Semitic messages were targeted at small shopkeepers.

The Nazis used posters, leaflets, rallies and speeches to disseminate their propaganda as well as modern technology such as radio and film. Rallies were designed to provoke an emotional response through the orchestration of image and sound. The Nazis also benefited from their association with the **DNVP** as their leader, Alfred Hugenberg, placed his media empire at the service of Nazi propagandists.

Hitler's appeal

Joseph Goebbels cultivated an image of Hitler as Germany's heroic saviour. At a time when politicians seemed weak and ineffective, this was very appealing. This 'Hitler myth' helped to gain support for Hitler and the Nazis. During the presidential election of 1932, Hitler ran against President Hindenburg. Hitler's campaign, 'Hitler over Germany', portrayed the Nazi leader as dynamic and modern as he harnessed modern technology to put his message across, and travelled innovatively via aeroplane during his campaign. Hitler came second in the election and established himself as a credible political leader.

Identify an argument

Below are a series of definitions, a sample exam-style question and two sample conclusions. One of the conclusions achieves a high level because it contains an argument. The other achieves a lower level because it contains only description and assertion. Identify which is which. The mark scheme on page 68 will help you.

- **Description:** a detailed account.
- **Assertion:** a statement of fact or an opinion which is not supported by a reason.
- **Reason:** a statement which explains or justifies something.
- **Argument:** an assertion justified with a reason.

How far do you agree that the increase in electoral support for the Nazi Party in the years 1928–1933 was the result of effective propaganda and electioneering?

Sample 1

The increase in electoral support for the Nazi Party 1928–1933 was partly the result of effective propaganda and electioneering. Messages in propaganda were tailored for different groups of people and this increased their effectiveness. Furthermore, Hitler's popularity was enhanced by propaganda and electioneering, and that increased electoral support for the Party. However, effective propaganda and electioneering only partly explains the Nazis' increase in support. Other factors include the depth of economic and political crisis in Germany 1929–1933. This crisis gave the Nazis an opportunity as it caused people to reject democracy and the Weimar Republic and turn to the Nazis. It also helped the Nazis gain support as they could say they had solutions. By effectively exploiting the Depression and political crisis through propaganda, the Nazis were able to increase their electoral support.

Sample 2

The increase in electoral support for the Nazi Party in the years 1928–1933 was partly the result of effective propaganda and electioneering. The Nazis had messages about bread, work and Jews. Hitler also fought the 1933 Presidential campaign with the slogan 'Hitler over Germany' and Joseph Goebbels organised campaigns for Hitler and created the idea of Hitler as a saviour for Germany. All of this helped the Nazis to gain support. Another factor was the Depression and political crisis which caused people to hate democracy. This also assisted the Nazis.

Develop the detail

Below are a sample exam-style question and a paragraph written in answer to this question. The paragraph contains a limited amount of detail. Annotate the paragraph to add additional detail to the answer.

How far do you agree that Hitler became chancellor in January 1933 primarily due to the electoral success of the Nazi Party?

The electoral success of the Nazi Party helped Hitler come to power in the sense that it made him a candidate to become chancellor. The Nazi Party's support grew substantially between the 1928 and the 1932 elections. The Party picked up support from people who did not like the Weimar Republic and this popularity made Hitler a candidate to be chancellor.

Hitler's appointment as chancellor

Revised

Support from a conservative elite

President Hindenburg resisted making Hitler chancellor after the July 1932 election despite the Nazis' electoral success. He offered Hitler the vice-chancellorship, but Hitler refused: he would hold out to be chancellor. Mass popularity was not enough for Hitler to be appointed. Crucially, it was the support he received from the political and economic elite that eventually led to his appointment:

- During 1932, a number of influential industrialists and bankers put pressure on Hindenburg to appoint Hitler chancellor. Those **lobbying** for Hitler included banker Hjalmar Schacht and the industrialists I.G. Farben and Gustav Krupp.
- Hitler benefited from von Papen's scheming against Chancellor von Schleicher, who was appointed in November 1932. Von Papen wanted to use Hitler's popular support to legitimise an authoritarian government. His own government had lacked this legitimacy in 1932. He worked with others such as Hindenburg's son Oscar and his state secretary, Otto Meissner, to persuade Hindenburg to appoint Hitler chancellor. Von Papen's plan involved his own appointment as vice-chancellor: Nazi members of the cabinet were to be a minority. He assumed he would be able to control Hitler: after Hitler's appointment, von Papen crowed, 'we've hired him'.
- As the economic and political crisis continued, many conservatives feared a communist takeover: the **KPD's** share of the vote increased from 3.2 million in 1928 to 5.9 million in November 1933. The Nazis' determination to smash the communists caused some conservatives to back Hitler.
- Many members of the conservative political and economic elite contributed to the Nazis' funds, including media baron and DNVP leader Alfred Hugenberg and steel manufacturer Fritz Thyssen.
- Von Schleicher's attempts to legitimise his government by working with the Nazis and the trade unions failed. Von Papen's government had completely failed to gain Reichstag support, and now so did von Schleicher's.

Hindenburg at this point finally relented and appointed Hitler. Though their vote share declined in the November 1932 election (from 37 to 32 per cent), the Nazis were still the largest party in the Reichstag.

German conservatives

German conservatives were from the old elite or the business class. They shared several aspects with the fascist Nazis, such as a hatred for **socialists** and communists, nationalist leanings and a desire for more authoritarian government.

Hitler's appointment to power

On 30 January 1933 Hitler was appointed chancellor of Germany, with von Papen as vice-chancellor, in a cabinet that contained only two other Nazi members.

Factors in Hitler's appointment to power

The **Great Depression** and politicians' failure to deal with it effectively gave Hitler an opportunity and caused more people to listen to his message. Many were profoundly disillusioned with Weimar democracy, which was not strongly **entrenched** and which never appeared to have actually worked. The Nazis saw their support rise dramatically during 1929–1930 until they were the most popular political party. Some conservatives saw the Nazis as a way of creating a populist authoritarian government. With their support, Hindenburg was eventually persuaded to appoint Hitler chancellor.

Other factors contributing to Hitler's appointment to power include: Hitler's personal role (as a charismatic leader and tactician), the impact of Nazi propaganda and SA violence.

You're the examiner

a

Below are a sample exam-style question and a paragraph written in answer to this question. Read the paragraph and the mark scheme provided on page 68. Decide which level you would award the paragraph. Write the level below, along with a justification for your decision.

How far was the primary reason for Hitler's appointment to power the support that he had from the conservative elite?

Hitler was partly appointed to power because he had the support of some conservatives such as von Papen. Von Papen persuaded Hindenburg to appoint Hitler to power. Von Papen thought he could use Hitler. In addition, Hitler had the support of some in the industrial elite such as Schacht and Farben. They wrote a letter to Hindenburg which said that Hitler should be appointed. The conservatives all helped Hitler.

Level: Reason for choosing this level:

Recommended reading

Below is a list of suggested further reading on this topic.

- *The Face of the Third Reich*, pages 53–69, Joachim C. Fest (1970)
- *From Kaiser to Führer: Germany 1900–1945*, pages 193–205, Geoff Layton (2009)
- *Fascism: A History*, pages 110–113, Roger Eatwell (1995)

Exam focus

Revised

Below is a sample A-grade essay. Read it and the examiner comments around it.

How far do you agree with the view that Hitler was appointed chancellor in January 1933 because he was leader of the most popular political party in Germany?

> The introduction begins by setting out a clear argument. This creates sustained analysis.

Hitler was leader of the most popular political party in Germany. This was clearly a significant factor in his appointment to power, as the Nazi Party's popularity made Hitler a candidate for chancellor. However, Hitler was also appointed to power because of the economic and political crisis that Germany experienced during 1929–1933, and because he had the support of powerful people in Germany.

> The essay begins by examining the factor given in the question. In so doing, it immediately focuses on the question.

By 1932 the Nazi Party was the most popular political party in Germany and this put Hitler in the running to be chancellor. In the July 1932 elections, the Nazi Party had gained 37.3 per cent of the vote and became the largest party in the Reichstag, while the Party's membership was huge: by early 1933, there were around 2 million members. The Nazi Party's and Hitler's popularity rose during the Great Depression in Germany as other politicians were seen to have failed and the Nazis promised solutions to Germany's difficulties. The popularity of the Party helped to establish Hitler as a credible political leader and forced Hindenburg to consider Hitler for the chancellorship. However, at a high point of the Nazi Party's popularity, after the elections of July 1932, President Hindenburg refused to appoint Hitler and was only prepared to offer him the vice-chancellorship. Clearly, the popularity of the Nazi Party on its own was not enough to see Hitler appointed because the appointment of the chancellor remained the decision of the president. Hitler came to power in January 1933 only after Hindenburg's mind had been changed by economic and political crisis and by members of the conservative elite in Germany.

> An explanation of the specific role of the factor is given.

> This paragraph raises the level of detail in the essay by using precise statisics.

The Depression in Germany created a political crisis that resulted in Hitler's appointment to power. By 1932, around one in three Germans of working age was unemployed. There had been 50,000 bankruptcies, a major banking crisis in 1931, and the economy had shrunk by 40 per cent. The continued failure of politicians such as von Papen to resolve these problems increased the likelihood that Hindenburg would eventually give Hitler the opportunity of power, as established politicians were seen to have failed to have provided solutions. Furthermore, the economic depression contributed to the unpopularity of von Papen and von Schleicher. This unpopularity was illustrated when von Papen lost a vote of no-confidence in the Reichstag in 1932. The Depression made the governments of Germany unpopular and weak. Therefore popularity did play a role in Hitler's appointment, as the appointment was an attempt to re-establish popular support for the government of Germany.

Finally, Hindenburg appointed Hitler partly because he was persuaded to do so by Germany's conservative elite. In autumn 1932 powerful businessmen and bankers, such as I.G. Farben and Hjalmar Schacht, wrote to Hindenburg and urged him to appoint Hitler. Von Papen himself, and some of those close to Hindenburg like his son, Oscar, also worked to persuade Hindenburg that Hitler should be appointed chancellor, in a government dominated by conservatives with von Papen as vice-chancellor. The conservatives turned to the Nazis because they feared communism and mistakenly believed they would be able to control Hitler. Clearly, without the support of the elites it is much less likely that Hitler would have been appointed chancellor, because they persuaded Hindenburg to choose Hitler.

This paragraph contains a high level of detail about the motives of specific individuals.

Overall, Hitler was partly appointed as chancellor because he was leader of the most popular party in Germany. It was this fact that made him a candidate for the job. Also, appointing Hitler as chancellor was a way of creating popular support for the government. However, this was not the only factor: at the point that the Nazis became the largest party in the Reichstag, President Hindenburg did not appoint Hitler. It was only after continued political problems, and with the backing of conservative elite, that Hindenburg actually appointed Hitler to power.

The conclusion puts forward the same argument as the introduction, and helps create sustained analysis by showing how the different factors relate to each other.

27/30

This response considers the precise role of the given factor very clearly. Two additional factors are examined, and supported with accurate detail. The answer is awarded a mark in Level 5 because the essay shows how all of the factors are linked and therefore creates sustained analysis. The answer could get a higher mark if it considered another factor in a similar way. The conclusion gives a considered argument.

Two types of question

Exam-style questions can take two forms:

- questions that require you to consider a range of different factors – either causes or consequences
- questions that require you to make a judgement about the impact of a single factor.

Answers to the first type of question need to consider a range of factors. Answers to the second type of question need to consider different aspects of a single factor.

The essay above answers the first type of question, and consequently addresses a range of factors that enabled Hitler to be appointed to power. The following question similarly relates to the rise of the Nazi Party, but is a single factor question. Draw a plan for your answer to this question.

How successfully did the Nazi Party increase their support between 1928 and 1932?

Section 3:
The Third Reich in action

Nazi economic solutions

Revised

The German economy in 1933

Germany's economy was still in serious trouble when the Nazis took over.

- The economy had shrunk by around 40 per cent.
- It is estimated that around 8 million people were unemployed.
- Demand for German products abroad remained low.
- The agricultural sector was still in recession.
- The banking sector was very weak: five major banks had collapsed in 1931.

Schacht, Mefo Bills and the New Plan

Finance Minister Hjalmar Schacht dominated Nazi economic policy during 1933–1936. His policies focused on job creation and stimulating economic growth. In agriculture, **Reich Food Estate** subsidies and tariffs on imported food helped farmers obtain reasonable prices for their produce. Under Schacht:

- public investment tripled, and government spending increased by 70 per cent between 1933 and 1936
- the Reich Labour Service employed 19 to 25 year olds which helped with the problem of youth unemployment
- public works schemes saw the construction of **autobahns**, houses and public buildings
- armaments schemes and agricultural schemes, such as land reclamation projects, also provided employment.

These measures were partly paid for by taxation, but Schacht also designed the **Mefo Bills** scheme to finance government spending. These were essentially government-produced IOUs which could be used by the government as a kind of extra currency to pay for spending. The recipients could exchange Mefo bills within five years for real money. Mefo Bills earned four per cent interest every year.

In his **New Plan** (September 1934), Schacht also tried to encourage German trade by establishing **bilateral** trading agreements with other countries such as Romania.

These policies were quite successful: unemployment fell to around 1.5 million by 1936 and production increased by around 90 per cent between 1932 and 1936. However, Schacht failed to solve Germany's **balance of payments** problem. Germany imported more than it exported, which created a shortage of foreign currency.

Goering, *Wehrwirtschaft* and the Four Year Plan

Despite Schacht's success, by 1936 he was falling out of favour with Hitler. With unemployment reduced and the economy growing, Hitler wanted to concentrate on creating a fearsome military machine. Hitler wished to create a war economy, a ***Wehrwirtschaft***, to prepare the country for fighting a major war. In contrast, Schacht wished to focus economic policy on developing exports to address the balance of payments problem. Senior Nazi and head of the **Luftwaffe** Hermann Goering was prepared to take the economy in the direction that Hitler wanted and in August 1936, Hitler gave Goering sweeping powers over the economy, appointing him **plenipotentiary** of the **Four Year Plan**.

The 1936 Four Year Plan: key features

- To fight a large war, Germany wanted to be **autarkic.** Therefore, the plan involved increased production in agriculture and raw materials, and **ersatz** materials to replace imports (such as the production of artificial rubber).
- Massive expansion of armaments was planned: a huge industrial enterprise was established (the Reichswerke Hermann Goering [RWHG]), to develop armaments production.

The Four Year Plan was partially successful. Massive expansion took place in rearmament, including areas such as the production of explosives, but autarky was not attained by 1939. Ersatz products were of inferior quality and a third of raw materials still had to be imported. Additionally, armaments production did not reach its targets.

Support or challenge

Below is a sample exam-style question, which asks how far you agree with a specific statement. Below this are a series of general statements which are relevant to the question. Using your own knowledge and the information on the opposite page decide whether these statements support or challenge the statement in the question and tick the appropriate box.

How accurate is it to say that Nazi economic policy was successful in the period 1933–1941?

	SUPPORT	CHALLENGE
Public investment tripled between 1933 and 1936.		
Ersatz goods were of inferior quality.		
Germany imported more than it exported.		
There were major public works projects, such as the autobahns.		
Unemployment fell.		
The Mefo Bills scheme allowed the government to invest.		
Autarky was not achieved.		

Identify an argument

Below are a series of definitions, a sample exam-style question and two sample conclusions. One of the conclusions achieves a high level because it contains an argument. The other achieves a lower level because it contains only description and assertion. Identify which is which. The mark scheme on page 68 will help you.

- **Description:** a detailed account.
- **Assertion:** a statement of fact or an opinion which is not support by a reason.
- **Reason:** a statement which explains or justifies something.
- **Argument:** an assertion justified with a reason.

How accurate is it to say that the Nazis were largely successful in achieving their economic aims between 1933–1939?

Sample 1

The Nazis achieved their aims in economic policy 1933–1939 to some extent. Unemployment was significantly reduced between 1933 and 1936. Furthermore, the Nazis were able to begin to create a Wehrwirtschaft, a key aim of theirs. However, in some crucial respects they did not achieve their aims. Autarky was not a success as imports continued to exceed exports, and ersatz products were often inferior. Overall, the Nazis had partial success in achieving their aims in economic policy.

Sample 2

In some ways the Nazis achieved their aims. They built autobahns, which were motorways, and also set up the Reichswerke Hermann Goering (RWHG), a huge military industrial company. Schacht also introduced Mefo Bills which companies would get for doing work for the government, to be exchanged later for real money. He also had the New Plan which helped Germany to build up its trade but didn't achieve autarky.

Volksgemeinschaft and social policies

Revised

The Nazis implemented policies to attempt to control and obtain the support of various social groups. They sought to unify so-called '**Aryans**' in Germany under the ideal of ***Volksgemeinschaft***.

> ### *Volksgemeinschaft*
>
> The Nazis wanted a racially pure *Volksgemeinschaft* ('national community'). Members would unify through Nazi ideology and German nationalism, and form a strong and racially pure Germany under key values such as '**blood and soil**'. The *Volksgemeinschaft* was supposed to overcome class-based divisions. 'Outsider' groups such as Jews, the disabled and vagrants were excluded.

The working class

The Nazis outlawed trades unions and banned the communist **KPD** and the socialist **SPD** which many **working-class** people supported during the Weimar years. A Nazi organisation, the *Deutsche Arbeitesfront* or DAF, was supposed to represent workers but instead set wages, disciplined workers and increased control over them. This made it easier to increase working hours during the 1930s: while overall wages grew (compared to 1932), earnings per hour did not. Health and safety standards also declined.

Despite the harder working conditions, and their reduced **bargaining power** caused by the destruction of trades unions, workers did benefit in some ways under the Nazis.

- Unemployment fell to 1.5 million by 1936.
- Poorer working-class families benefited from policies that increased benefits to larger families.
- The **Beauty of Labour Scheme** worked to improve the physical appearance of workplaces.
- The **Strength Through Joy (KdF)** scheme allowed some workers and their families to enjoy more leisure activities. For example, 28,500 workers for Siemens in Berlin took a holiday due to the programme. However, KdF's most famous project, the production of a people's car (the *Volkswagen*), was largely a propaganda stunt. In reality, the scheme did not really get off the ground.

Some working-class Germans joined secret opposition movements, such as the **SOPADE** network of the SPD and the communist organisation, **Rot Kappelle**. Evidence also suggests that many ordinary working people engaged in low level **non-conformity**, which suggests they were not convinced about all aspects of Nazism and thus not fully part of the *Volksgemeinschaft*.

Peasants and farmers

The Nazi regime idealised peasants and farmers as the embodiment of traditional German values and racial purity. The Nazis assisted farmers by including tariffs on imports to help maintain prices, writing off debts and setting easily payable mortgage rates. However, many small farmers grew to resent the Reich Food Estate (see page 36). Larger landowners generally acquiesced with the regime, relieved that their land was not redistributed.

The *mittelstand*

The lower middle class of small businessmen, tradesmen and craftsmen had long felt threatened by industrialisation, mass production and big business. They were susceptible to **anti-Semitic** messages about the supposed damage of 'Jewish' capital. The Nazis claimed to represent the *Mittelstand* and protected them with measures such as trade regulations, though ultimately they required big business to develop their war economy and so the *Mittelstand* were in reality neglected.

Big business

Many big businesses benefited from Nazi rule. The expansion of the economy through public works, Mefo Bills and the huge expansion of the war economy benefited the manufacturing, arms production and chemicals industries. The value of the German stock exchange increased by 250 per cent between 1932 and 1940.

Mind map

Use the information on the opposite page to add detail to the mind map below.

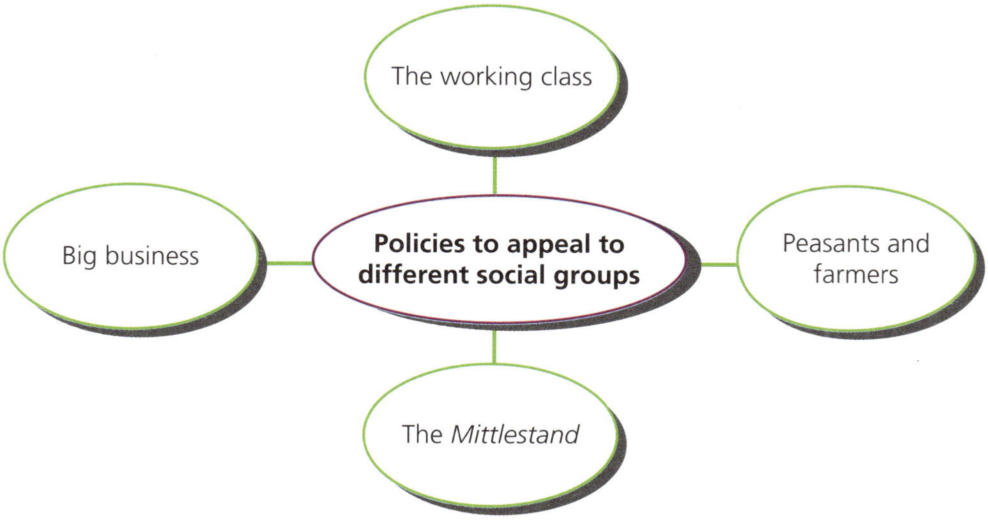

Develop the detail

Below are a sample exam-style question and a paragraph written in answer to this question. The paragraph contains a limited amount of detail. Annotate the paragraph to add additional detail to the answer.

How far did the Nazis create a *Volksgemeinschaft* in Germany between 1933–1941?

The Nazis were partially successful in creating a Volksgemeinschaft. One way in which the Nazis tried to do this was through introducing policies to appeal to different social groups. So, for example, there were policies to appeal to the working class and to peasants and farmers. These policies contributed to the Nazis' partial success in creating a Volksgemeinschaft.

Revised

Racial policies

The 'racial' strength of 'Aryan' Germans was viewed as the key to establishing a strong Germany. Groups seen as harmful to German racial strength were classed as 'outsiders' and subject to persecution. In Nazi Germany, the doctrine of **Aryan racial supremacy** had dangerous consequences for Jews and other people who did not fit into the Nazis' conception of a master race. The ultimate result was **genocide** and mass murder during the Second World War.

The *Einsatzgruppen*

These were SS **death squads** which followed the German army as Germany conquered eastern Europe and the Soviet Union, carrying out mass killings of ideological and 'racial' enemies.

Policies towards other outsider groups

Other groups excluded from the *Volksgemeinschaft* included:

- Political enemies such as communists and **socialists**: around 150,000 **left-wing** enemies of the Nazis were imprisoned during 1933–1934.
- Gypsies (Roma and Sinti): this group were the first to be murdered because of their 'racial' identity. When the Second World War broke out, German gypsies were deported to Poland.
- Disabled people: the Law for the Prevention of Hereditarily Diseased Offspring (1933) permitted compulsory sterilisation for those with hereditary conditions. In 1939, the **Aktion T4** scheme was launched, in which disabled children (and later adults) were murdered.
- Homosexuals: gay people were subject to Nazi persecution partly because they were viewed as resisting the Nazi desire for all Aryans to breed. In 1936, a Reich Central Office for the Combating of Homosexuality was established. Approximately 15,000 German gay people were imprisoned in camps.
- A-socials: people who did not conform to Nazi social ideals were classed as 'a-social' from the mid 1930s, and often imprisoned in concentration camps. These included the homeless and alcoholics.

Timeline: persecution of Jews in Europe

Year	Persecution affecting Jews
1933	• 1 April – boycott of Jewish shops • April – all Jews (except war veterans) are removed from the civil service
1935	• September – The **Nuremburg Laws** ban 'intermarriage'; Jews' German citizenship is removed
1938	• March – violent attacks on Jews and Jewish property following **Anschluss**; 45,000 Austrian Jews are forced to emigrate • November – **Kristallnacht**: anti-Jewish attacks on thousands of businesses and synagogues; 20,000 Jewish men are sent to **concentration camps** • Aryanisation begins: Jewish property is seized; Jews are banned from German economic life
1939	• January – Reich Central Office for Emigration is established to promote emigration of Jews out of Europe • September – Germany invades Poland and the Second World War starts; ghettos for Polish Jews are established • October – German Jews are placed under curfew
1940	• The Madagascar Plan is drawn up: a plan to move 4 million European Jews to live in Madagascar. The idea was eventually abandoned as impractical.
1941	• All Jews are forced to wear the **Star of David**. • June: following the invasion of the **Soviet Union, *Einsatzgruppen*** and their local supporters carry out systematic massacres of Jews
1942	• January – the Wannsee Conference: representatives of various party and state organisations agree to the '**Final Solution**'. • Spring – death camps are established at Belzec, Sobibor, Treblinka and Auschwitz.
1942–1944	• Transportation of Jews from all over Europe to death camps. Ultimately around 6 million Jews were murdered during the **Holocaust**, of whom around 1 million were murdered in *Einsatzgruppen* massacres.

Simple essay style

Below is a sample exam-style question. Use your own knowledge and the information on the opposite page to produce a plan for this question. Choose four general points, and provide three specific pieces of information to support each general point. Once you have planned your essay, write the introduction and conclusion for the essay. The introduction should list the points to be discussed in the essay. The conclusion should summarise the key points and justify which point was the most important.

Why did Nazi policies towards racial minorities, including the Jewish people, change in the years 1933–1945?

RAG – Rate the timeline

Below are a sample exam-style question and a timeline. Read the question, study the timeline and, using three coloured pens, put a red, amber or green star next to the events to show:

- **red** – events and policies that have no relevance to the question.
- **amber** – events and policies that have some significance to the question.
- **green** – events and policies that are directly relevant to the question.

How accurate is it to say that there were few changes in the Nazis' policies towards the Jewish people in the period 1933–1945?

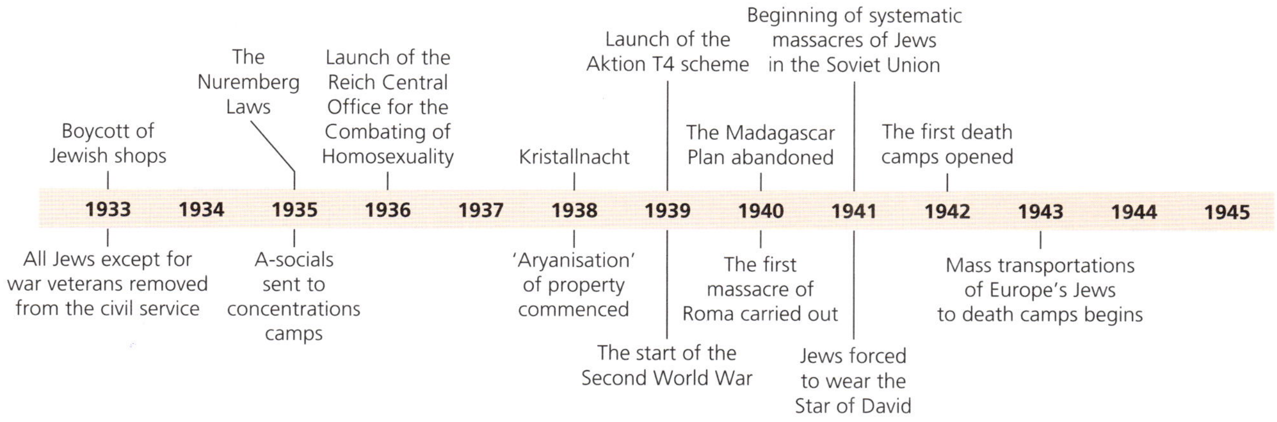

Policies towards women

Revised

Nazi ideas about women

The Nazis believed that men and women should have completely different roles. Their view was that women should not work. Nazi officials said that women should focus upon their traditional role as homemakers and child bearers. Women's role should be that of *Kinder, Küche, Kirche* (children, kitchen and the Church). The Nazi attitude partly resulted from a desire to build a healthy master race and so it was felt that the birth rate must increase. At the same time, reducing the number of working women would, it was believed, increase male employment.

Nazi policies

Nazi policies towards women were aimed at promoting marriage, births and women's traditional role (thus reducing female employment).

- Married couples could take out loans which were partially converted into gifts upon the birth of each child.
- Maternity benefits and family allowances were improved, and taxes reduced for those with children.
- Contraception advice was restricted and anti-abortion laws enforced.
- Propaganda promoted idealised images of mothers and honorary crosses were awarded to those with large families (eight children would get you a gold cross).
- To reduce female employment, women were banned from working in many professional jobs such as medicine and law. Women who left employment to get married could obtain an interest free loan of 600 **marks**. Propaganda campaigns encouraged women to leave employment, and employers and **labour exchanges** to favour men.
- Women were restricted to only 10 per cent of university places.

The results of Nazi policies towards women

The results of Nazi policies in this area were mixed. The birth rate rose from 14.7 per 1000 Germans in 1933 to 20.3 in 1939, and the proportion of women in the labour force decreased from 37 per cent to 33 per cent in 1939. However, the number of women in work increased as the labour force in Germany expanded during this time: rapid rearmament was not feasible without female labour. Measures to restrict female employment affected only small numbers of middle-class, educated women. Additionally, the rate of marriages did not increase significantly during the 1930s. Where the Nazis achieved their aims (in a rising birth rate, for example) it is difficult to establish whether this was because of their polices or down to other factors, such as rising prosperity, which may have encouraged people to have more children.

Nazi Women's organisations

Women were barred from most areas of the Nazi Party ruling structures, but could participate in the National Socialist Womanhood (NSF) and the German Women's Enterprise (DFW). These organisations were not designed to encourage female participation in politics, however: they existed to promote Nazi ideology regarding women's role.

Spectrum of significance

Below are a sample exam-style question and a list of general points which could be used to answer the question. Use your general knowledge and the information on the opposite page to reach a judgement about the importance of these general points to the question posed. Write numbers on the spectrum below to indicate their relative importance. Having done this, write a brief justification of your placement, explaining why some of these factors are more important than others. The resulting diagram could form the basis of an essay plan.

How far did the Nazis achieve the aims of their policies towards women?

1. The birth rate rose.
2. The marriage rate remained constant.
3. Middle-class women were removed from professional jobs.
4. The proportion of women in the workforce was reduced, but the overall number of women working increased.
5. Fewer women went to university.

Aims not achieved at all ⟷ Aims totally achieved

Introducing an argument

Below are a sample exam question, a list of key points to be made in the essay, and a simple introduction and conclusion for the essay. Read the question, the plan, and the introduction and conclusion. Rewrite the introduction and conclusion in order to develop an argument.

How far did the lives of women in Nazi Germany change in the years 1933–1939?

Key points

- Changes in employment and education.
- Changes in family policy.
- Propaganda and Nazi ideology.
- The impact of Nazi policies on Jewish women and other outsider groups of women.

Introduction

The lives of women in Nazi Germany changed to some extent under the Nazis. The Nazis had policies that affected women in the areas of employment, education and family, and Nazi ideas about women also had an impact.

Conclusion

There were many changes affecting women in Nazi Germany and their lives changed to an extent. For example, there were changes in employment for middle-class women and in family policies.

Policies towards children and education

Revised

For the Nazis, children were central to providing the future master race.

Nazi ideas about children and education

The Nazis felt that:

- children could and should be **indoctrinated** in Nazi ideas
- education should be harnessed to serve the state and Nazi ideology
- children should be conscripted into the movement to build it and provide future soldiers and mothers.

Nazi educational policies

In 1933, Jewish teachers considered politically dubious were sacked. Remaining teachers were encouraged to join a Nazi Teachers' League and go on re-training schemes. By 1938, 60 per cent of teachers had participated in these programmes. Nazi attitudes were encouraged in schools: people performed the **Hitler Salute** and promoted anti-Semitic ideas. From 1935, the curriculum was altered to reflect Nazi values: teachers taught a **nationalist** version of German history and focused on Nazi racial ideas, such as their racial hierarchy and **eugenics**, in biology. The Party had to approve all textbooks. The curriculum also enforced traditional gender roles, with boys taking part in tough physical training and girls taking cookery classes.

In addition, the Nazis established new schools to train the future Nazi elite:

- From 1936 the SS ran military-style boarding schools. By 1938 there were 28 of these.
- Three so-called 'Order Castles' were created to train those considered as future leaders.

Nazi Youth Organisations

Youth organisations were designed to indoctrinate children in Nazi ideology and train them for their roles in Nazi Germany. Overall membership of Hitler Youth rose from 100,000 in 1933 to 6 million by 1936.

- The Hitler Youth (HJ), for boys aged 10–18 years old, was formed in 1926. The HJ offered activities such as hiking, camping and, increasingly, military training. By 1937, 1 million boys had participated in HJ youth camps. Though membership became compulsory in March 1939, its increasing militarisation reduced its popularity during the Second World War.
- The League of German Maidens (BDM) organised sporting activities and camping trips for girls, as well as training to become future homemakers. By 1937, 100,000 girls had attended a BDM youth camp. During the war, BDM members volunteered to help with charity collections and in hospitals. Later, BDM members were involved in anti-aircraft activities.

The impact of Nazi policies towards children and education

Nazi policies caused educational standards to decline, partly because the curriculum had been hijacked by ideology and partly because the regime emphasised physical fitness over intellectual achievements. Reports suggest that discipline in schools declined. Nazi youth organisations did provide children with expanded opportunities to participate in sport, social activities, and travel in the German countryside, and the organisations were popular. However, their increasingly compulsory and regimented nature alienated those who had initially been attracted by the sense that the Nazis represented a rebellion against established values. Some young people were actively involved in groups that rejected Nazism, most notably the **Edelweiss Pirates**.

Young anti-Nazi groups

The Edelweiss Pirates were an explicitly anti-Nazi youth group. They wore banned uniforms and attacked the Hitler Youth while also holding their own activities for young people. The **Swing Youth** were non-conformists who listened to American jazz, dressed in an unconventional manner and engaged in rebellious behaviour. The Nazi regime treated both of these groups as a threat and members of both the Edelweiss Pirates and the Swing Youth were arrested.

Delete as applicable

Below are a sample exam-style question and a paragraph written in answer to this question. Read the paragraph and decide which of the possible options (underlined) is the most appropriate. Delete the least appropriate options and complete the paragraph by justifying your selection.

How far did the lives of young people change in Germany 1933–1939?

In terms of education, the lives of young people in Germany 1933–1939 changed <u>completely/to a great extent/partially/to a limited extent</u>. In schools, the curriculum was heavily controlled by the Nazis after 1935 and all textbooks had to be approved by the Nazis. The Nazis used education as a means of spreading their ideology, and so for example, their racial theories were taught in biology, and anti-Semitic ideas were promoted. Nazi ideology about the roles of men and women was also promoted, as was a nationalistic view of German history. In addition, the Nazis removed teachers who were considered to be politically hostile to them from schools to try to control what students were being taught. The Nazis' educational policies had a <u>significant/moderate/limited</u> impact on young people in Nazi Germany in the sense that

You're the examiner

Below are a sample exam-style question and a paragraph written in answer to this question. Read the paragraph and the mark scheme provided on page 68. Decide which level you would award the paragraph. Write the level below, along with a justification for your decision.

How far did the Nazis achieve the aims of their policies towards young people?

The Nazis achieved the aims of their policies towards young people to a large extent. In education, the Nazis succeeded in taking over the curriculum which allowed them to indoctrinate children. After 1935, the Nazis controlled textbook content. In history, German nationalist ideas were taught, and in biology, Nazi racial theories were promoted. The Nazis also advanced their ideas about the roles of men and women in lessons in schools. The Nazis helped to ensure that children in schools did not receive any information that contradicted their ideas by removing teachers from their jobs who were politically opposed to the Nazis.

Level: Reason for choosing this level:

Exam focus

Revised

Below is a sample Level 4 essay. Read it and the examiner comments around it.

How far did the Nazis create a *Volksgemeinschaft* in Germany between 1933–1941?

A clear answer to the question: this is an effective introduction.

The Nazis were partially successful in creating a Volksgemeinschaft in Germany between 1933 and 1941. They were particularly successful in inspiring many children with their vision of a national community. They also created schemes such as KdF that appealed to ordinary people. However, not everyone in Germany felt part of the Volksgemeinschaft.

Rather than simply providing a for and against argument, this essay considers a number of different ways in which the Nazis did or did not create a *Volksgemeinschaft*.

The Nazis were in some ways successful in creating a Volksgemeinschaft. They focused particular attention on trying to indoctrinate young people and integrate them into the 'national community'. A sign that the Nazis had some success with this is the fact that numbers in the Hitler Youth rose enormously even before membership of the organisation had been made compulsory: from 100,000 in 1933 to 1 million in 1936. There were high levels of participation among boys and girls. By 1937, 1 million boys aged between 10 and 18 had participated in Hitler Youth camps and 100,000 girls had attended League of German Maidens youth camps. The fact that, by 1935, education had been transformed so that Nazi ideology was promoted in schools may have helped the Nazis to convince young people to support them and contributed to creating a Volksgemeinschaft. Clearly, the Nazis were broadly successful in creating a Volksgemeinschaft among young German people as boys and girls were indoctrinated with Nazi ideas at school and gained a sense of unity through participating in Nazi youth groups.

This paragraph uses detailed statistics to support the point.

The Nazis also partially created a Volkgemeinschaft through their policies targeted at various social groups. So, for example, poorer families benefited from increased benefits and workers benefited from the Strength through Joy (KdF) scheme, which provided holidays and excursions for people, including cruises on the Baltic. For example, 28,500 workers for Siemens in Berlin took a holiday due to the programme. Furthermore, the Nazis sought to create a Volksgemeinschaft in their policies towards women. Marriage loans and maternity benefits helped to create a sense of national community for many women. These policies led to some successes. For example, the birth rate rose from 14.7 per 1000 Germans in 1933 to 20.3 in 1939. What is more, the proportion of women in the labour force decreased from 37 per cent to 33 per cent in 1939. Peasants and farmers were shown in Nazi propaganda as important to Nazi ideas and were helped by policies which allowed them to write off debts and gain cheap mortgages. Overall, the Nazis had some success in creating a Volkgemeinschaft among workers, women and peasants because programmes such as the KdF helped people to feel included and therefore unite behind the Nazis.

The paragraph concludes with clear analysis evaluating how far the Nazis had created a *Volksgemeinschaft.*

However, the Nazis did not succeed in unifying all 'Aryan' Germans in a Volksgemeinschaft. Some people in Nazi Germany opposed the Nazis. Some young people were anti-Nazi, such as the members of the Edelweiss Pirates. Many peasants resented the interference of the Reich Food Estate. Not everyone benefited from the Nazi regime and that may have counted against the formation of a Volksgemeinschaft. Working-class people's independent trades unions were shut down and there was a widespread recognition that the Deutsche Arbeitesfront (DAF), which the Nazis set up to represent the workers, was unable to deliver better wages or working conditions. A few people also participated in opposition organisations such as SOPADE. Consequently, the Nazis failed to create a completely unified Volksgemeinschaft as some young people, workers and peasants were dissatisfied with aspects of the Nazi regime rather than united behind Nazi values.

This paragraph correctly links the idea of *Volksgemeinschaft* to the 'Aryan race'.

Overall, the Nazis created a Volksgemeinschaft to some extent, but not everyone was unified behind the Nazis. The Nazis were particularly successful in getting young people involved with and supportive of the regime and also had policies which appealed to the working class and women. However, as not everyone benefited from Nazi rule they failed to unify 'Aryans' of all classes behind the values of the Nazi movement.

The conclusion offers a focused summary of the essay and a clear judgement. Like the introduction it could be improved by linking its judgement to a clear definition of a *Volksgemeinschaft.*

24/30

This is an effective essay, in which various points are advanced to support the argument that the Nazis were only partially successful in creating a Volksgemeinschaft. There is a good range and depth of accurate evidence. However, the essay lacks the sustained analysis that would gain the essay a mark in Level 5. It could be improved by defining a Volksgemeinschaft and by linking back to this definition in each paragraph.

Moving from Level 4 to Level 5

The Exam Focus at the end of Section 2 provided a Level 5 essay. The essay here achieves a Level 4. Read both essays, and the examiner's comments provided. Make a list of the additional features required to push a Level 4 essay into Level 5.

Section 4: The fall of the Third Reich

An overview of the Second World War

Revised

On 1 September 1939, Nazi Germany invaded Poland. On 3 September, Britain and France declared war on Germany and the Second World War began.

The causes of the Second World War

Hitler's aggressive foreign policy

Hitler sought ***lebensraum***. By September 1939, he had already expanded the German military and annexed Austria and Czechoslovakia. Britain and France decided to act when Germany invaded Poland because they felt they could not allow Germany to become excessively dominant.

A weak international system

Hitler was able to ignore the Treaty of Versailles and launch aggressive actions because the international system was weak in the 1930s:

- The USA and **USSR** were both **isolationist**.
- Britain and France were not in a strong position to uphold international order as they both had problems resulting from the Depression.
- Keen to avoid war, and feeling that the Treaty of Versailles was excessively harsh, Britain followed a policy of **appeasement** which may have encouraged Hitler's aggression.
- Concerted action between the USSR, France and Britain might have prevented Hitler's attack on Poland but the three countries could not work together: eventually the USSR signed the **Nazi–Soviet Pact** which allowed Poland to be carved up between themselves and Germany. Hitler could now attack Poland without fear of Soviet opposition.

The course of the war

German successes: 1939–1941

After the Nazis had overrun Poland using ***Blitzkrieg***, a period of **phoney war** began. This was broken by the invasion of Scandinavia in March 1940 where the British navy unsuccessfully engaged the Germans near the coast of Norway. Subsequently, Germany conquered the **Low Countries** in quick succession before defeating the British and French armies to take control of France by June 1940.

After failing to push Britain out of the war during the **Battle of Britain** in summer 1940, Hitler launched an invasion of the **Soviet Union**, **Operation Barbarossa**, in June 1941. Initially, this attack met with considerable success as the ***Wehrmacht*** rapidly seized large amounts of territory. Meanwhile, German forces engaged the **Allies** in North Africa. Invasion of the Soviet Union and the ensuing huge and prolonged campaign required Germany to direct all the resources to the war effort: it was now, in Goebbels' phrase, 'total war'.

The tide turns: Late 1941–1943

With the USA now in the war (following the Japanese attack on **Pearl Harbor** in December 1941), the Germans started to struggle. In North Africa, British forces defeated the German army at El Alamein in November 1942, while in the Soviet Union the Germans suffered a serious defeat at Stalingrad in January 1943. From here on, the **Red Army** started to defeat the *Wehrmacht*, and from May the Allies started to win the **Battle of the Atlantic**.

Defeat: 1944–1945

After defeating the Italian forces, US, British and Canadian forces had a second **front** in Italy and then opened up a third front in Northern France on **D-Day**, 6 June 1944, pushing the Germans back from the west. At the same time the Soviet Union had a string of successes in **Operation Bagration**. It was now only a matter of time until the Nazis were totally defeated. On 30 April 1945, when Soviet soldiers reached Berlin (see page 56), Hitler committed suicide. The European war was over.

Mind map

Use the information on the opposite page to add detail to the mind map below.

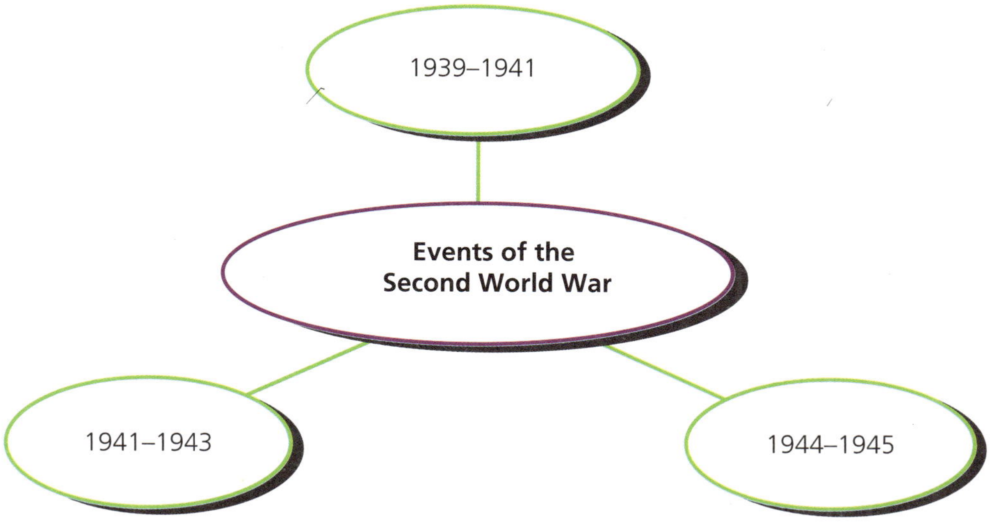

Recommended reading

Below is a list of suggested further reading on this topic.

- *Hitler, 1936–45: Nemesis*, pages 751–95, Ian Kershaw (2000)
- *The German Dictatorship*, pages 495–586, Karl Dietrich Bracher (1991)
- *Hitler: A Study in Tyranny* (Abridged Edition), pages 321–484, Alan Bullock (1971)

The economic impact of the war

Revised

Fighting the war placed enormous strains on the German economy and labour force.

The German economy during the early part of the war

Early on in the war, Hitler sought to dramatically expand the German war economy. Between 1939 and 1941, German military expenditure doubled. By 1941, 55 per cent of the workforce was involved in war-related projects. Despite these efforts, however, German productivity was disappointing and below that of rival countries. Britain produced twice as many aircraft as Germany in 1941, and the USSR 2600 more tanks. The chaotic organisation of the Nazi state hindered economic efficiency. The various bodies responsible, such as the Office of the **Four Year Plan**, **The Todt Organisation** and the Ministry of Armaments, did not co-ordinate effectively.

The appointment of Speer

To try to resolve these difficulties, Fritz Todt, head of the Ministry of Armaments, simplified the production of armaments in January 1942. Industry was now directed to increase productivity. Hitler sought to further improve matters by appointing Albert Speer as Minister of Munitions following Todt's death in February 1942. In September 1943, Speer's powers were extended when he was given responsibility for all industry and raw materials as Minister for Armaments and Production.

Speer's actions included:

- establishing a Central Planning Board to co-ordinate economic organisation
- encouraging the employment of women (although Hitler would never allow the complete **conscription** of women)
- using **concentration camp** prisoners as labour
- preventing the conscription of skilled workers
- deploying production lines
- promoting the standardisation of armaments and setting up an Armaments Commission to oversee this.

Speer's actions were successful. Ammunition production rose by 97 per cent, tank production rose by 25 per cent and total arms production by 59 per cent. Between 1942 and 1944 German war production trebled. Raw materials were also used more efficiently and munitions productivity per worker increased by 60 per cent.

The failures of the war economy

Although German production levels increased, the USA and the Soviet Union produced more. In the end, despite the improvements in efficiency Speer had put in place, the failures of the war economy contributed to Germany's defeat. There are a number of reasons for this:

- The war economy was not effectively co-ordinated. For example, some of the local party bosses, ***Gauleiter***, acted against the interests of economic efficiency.
- Labour shortages held the economy back:
  - Women were not as effectively mobilised as in the Soviet Union and Britain because Nazi ideology did not support female employment.
  - There was a heavy reliance upon foreign workers (of whom there were 6.4 million by 1942). These were often little more than badly treated and malnourished slave labourers; as a result their productivity was 60 to 80 per cent lower than that of the average German worker.
- Shortages of raw materials such as coal and oil was a problem: the production of **ersatz** materials did not fully resolve this and these products were often of inferior quality.
- The Germans needed the raw materials of the countries that they conquered, but the destruction they wreaked did not help them exploit these resources fully.
- In the Soviet Union, Stalin's **scorched earth policy** hindered the Nazis.
- Allied bombing reduced the capacity of the German economy to expand further.

Complete the paragraph

Below are a sample exam-style question and a paragraph written in answer to this question. The paragraph contains a point and specific examples, but lacks a concluding explanatory link back to the question. Complete the paragraph adding this link in the space provided.

Why did Germany lose the Second World War?

The failings of Nazi economic policies contributed to some extent to the defeat of Germany in the Second World War. There was a lack of effective co-ordination in the war economy and the actions of Gauleiter often worked against economic efficiency. In addition, the Nazis relied heavily upon foreign workers, of whom there were 6.4 million by 1942. Foreign workers were often underfed, badly treated and their productivity was low: 60–80 per cent less than that of the average German worker. Furthermore, because of Nazi ideology, women were not always effectively mobilised.

Support or challenge?

Below is a sample exam-style question which asks how far you agree with a specific statement. Below this are a series of general statements that are relevant to the question. Using your own knowledge and the information on the opposite page decide whether these statements support or challenge the statement in the question and tick the appropriate box.

'Nazi economic policies were successful in the period 1939–1945.' How far do you agree with this statement?

	SUPPORT	CHALLENGE
The war economy was chaotically organised.		
Speer improved the level of productivity.		
The actions of *Gauleiter* sometimes hindered economic efficiency.		
Women were not effectively mobilised.		
Speer improved the co-ordination of armaments production.		
The Germans lacked raw materials during the Second World War.		
Ersatz goods were inferior.		

The social impact of the war

Revised

The impact of the Second World War on ordinary Germans was profound and affected different social groups in different ways.

The impact on workers

- At the start of the war, to try to maximise the productivity of German workers, bonuses and overtime payments were banned, and wages were reduced. This strategy backfired, however, as there was then a higher level of **absenteeism**. Consequently, wage levels were restored by October 1939.
- The regime also sought to improve its mobilisation of labour by transferring workers in non-essential work to war work, and by creating a register of men and women who were of working age.
- As the war dragged on into 1944, the impact on German workers became severe, as holidays were banned and the working week became 60 hours. Workers were in a weak position to resist these new pressures.
- Workers were also kept in line via the system of organising them into groups overseen by a loyal party member.

Women

- While men were conscripted, married women with young children were often left alone to manage the home and domestic shortages.
- Nazi ideology emphasised the role of women as mothers and homemakers. Despite labour shortages, Hitler refused to authorise the mass conscription of women. Even though the power to conscript women existed, it was not much used.
- Women did not voluntarily join the workforce in large numbers because families of conscripts received reasonable benefits: the numbers of women employed in industry actually decreased between 1939 and 1941.
- The demands of total war required an adjustment in Nazi policy towards women: from January 1943, all women aged between 17 and 45 were required to register to work (though there were exemptions for pregnant women, those with two or more children, and farmer's wives). Necessity forced Hitler to modify, yet not entirely abandon, his policies towards women.
- Later, Hitler was persuaded to increase the upper age limit of working women to 50, which increased the number of women workers significantly. By 1945, 60 per cent of workers were women and women undertook some military duties such as anti-aircraft operations.

Youth

- While membership of the Hitler Youth and BDM had become compulsory, the Nazi regime did not conscript the young in the early period of the war.
- There was, however, great emphasis within the Hitler Youth on training boys to become future soldiers.
- One impact of the war on some young people was evacuation from cities such as Berlin and Hamburg that were affected by bombing after September 1940.
- The requirements of total war saw young people more directly involved in the war effort: 2 million youths were organised to help with the harvest in 1942, while the age of conscription was reduced to 17 in 1943.
- The **Waffen SS** trained some members of the Hitler Youth; 16 to 18 year olds were recruited into the organisation from 1943, and the age of conscription in other areas of the armed forces was reduced to 16 in 1945.
- By the end of the war, boys as young as 12 were deployed on the home front to use anti-tank weapons and so were involved in direct combat with Soviet forces.

Simple essay style

Below is a sample exam-style question. Use your own knowledge and the information on the opposite page to produce a plan for this question. Choose four general points, and provide three pieces of specific information to support each general point. Once you have planned your essay, write the introduction and conclusion for the essay. The introduction should list the points to be discussed in the essay. The conclusion should summarise the key points and justify which point was the most important.

To what extent did the lives of German citizens worsen during the years 1939–1945?

Identify an argument

Below are a series of definitions, a sample exam question and two sample conclusions. One of the conclusions achieves a high level because it contains an argument. The other achieves a lower level because it contains only description and assertion. Identify which is which. The mark scheme on page 68 will help you.

- **Description**: a detailed account.
- **Assertion**: a statement of fact or an opinion which is not supported by a reason.
- **Reason**: a statement which explains or justifies something.
- **Argument**: an assertion justified with a reason.

To what extent did living standards in Germany decline in the period 1939–1945?

Sample 1

Living standards in Germany declined significantly in the period 1939–1945. Workers' hours increased to 60 per week, and holidays were banned. Women had to cope with shortages of food and other goods. City bombing damaged many cities and some young people had to leave their homes.

Sample 2

Living standards in Germany declined to a significant extent in the period 1939–1945. Conditions at work harmed some people's standard of living as people worked very long hours, while shortages of food and other goods also affected people's lives. However, the standard of living did not collapse entirely: there were food rations available until the end of the war.

Politics and propaganda during wartime

Revised

The Nazis felt that keeping morale high was very important to the war effort and wanted to avoid the extreme shortages of food seen during the First World War. They also directed propaganda efforts at maintaining support for the work.

Attitudes and morale 1939–1942

Several measures helped maintain support for the regime early on in the war:

- While meat was rationed, it remained at the reasonable level of 500g per week until April 1942 and increased again in October.
- Early victories in Poland, Norway, Denmark, Luxembourg, Belgium and France helped maintain morale.
- Propaganda may also have had an impact, although intelligence reports indicate that support for the war was variable.

'Total War', propaganda and morale 1943–1945

The initial success of Barbarossa boosted morale but its difficulties produced a more negative mood. After 1942 people began to criticise Hitler's leadership, and **non-conformity** and cynicism were rife. In 1943, the regime could not cover up defeat at Stalingrad as the scale of the losses was so great. The high rate of casualties on the **Eastern Front** damaged morale and provoked some criticism of Hitler, who by this point rarely appeared in public. Goebbels was much more the public face of the regime from 1943.

Goebbels continued his efforts to maintain morale by urging perseverance, famously calling upon a crowd to support 'total war' at the **Sportpalast** in Berlin in February 1943. Films such as *The Adventures of Baron Munchausen* (1943) and *Kolberg* (1945) tried to encourage patriotic feeling, yet morale continued to fall. For example, in the Hitler Youth, many were disaffected. Factors which weakened support for the regime and morale included:

- difficult working conditions
- increasing shortages. By 1945, food shortages left many people hungry. Clothing, footwear and luxury goods were also in short supply. Some items, such as magazines and sweets, were not available at all
- allied bombing of German cities seems to have weakened morale in some areas
- the Soviet advance from 1943 worried the German public who feared Russian invasion
- the failure of the **V1 and V2** in a 1944 rocket campaign against South Eastern England and Allied ports like Antwerp.

Bombing

From 1940, the British had bombed industrial and military targets in Germany from aircraft, but by 1943 they had extended their targets to include civilian areas. The Americans joined these attacks. On 16 May 1943, the famous **Dambusters** raid (officially called Operation Chastise) was launched over the Ruhr. This damaged or destroyed around 100 factories as well as several power plants, and over 30 bridges, but German industry in this area recovered within a few months. In Hamburg, in July 1943, air raids caused a hugely destructive firestorm and damaged the industrial capabilities of the city. While air raids did not deliver a knockout blow to German capabilities and morale, they did seriously hinder the German war effort and provided distinct advantages to the Allies. For example, the Germans redeployed fighter aircraft away from the Eastern Front back to Germany to help with air defence. In total, bombing by the Allies killed 305,000 people, injured 780,000 and destroyed 2 million homes in Germany. The morality of the bombing of German civilians has been questioned: tens of thousands were killed by firestorms that engulfed Hamburg in 1943 and Dresden in 1945 after bombing raids.

Delete as applicable

a

Below are a sample exam-style question and a paragraph written in answer to this question. Read the paragraph and decide which of the possible options (underlined) is most appropriate. Delete the least appropriate options and complete the paragraph by justifying your selection.

How far do you agree that allied bombing campaigns were the main cause of the German defeat in the Second World War?

German defeat in the Second World War was significantly/partly/to a limited extent due to the impact of Allied bombing campaigns. Air raids did hinder the German war effort by destroying buildings and infrastructure, such as during Operation Chastise in 1943. Military and industrial sites were targeted. In addition, the bombing campaigns hindered the German war effort through the damage to morale that some of the bombing raids targeted at civilians caused. Around 1 million people were killed and injured in these raids. However, Allied bombing campaigns did not deliver a decisive blow against Germany: they contributed significantly/partly/to a limited extent to German defeat in the sense that

____

____

Develop the detail

a

Below are a sample exam-style question and a paragraph written in answer to this question. The paragraph contains a limited amount of detail. Annotate the paragraph to add additional detail to the answer.

How far do you agree that morale was effectively maintained in Germany during the Second World War?

Propaganda helped to maintain morale in Germany during the Second World War to some extent. The Nazis used propaganda for this purpose and Goebbels produced a number of films with a patriotic message. After 1943, Goebbels redoubled his propaganda efforts and urged the Germans to fight on in a famous speech. Whilst propaganda did help the Nazis to maintain morale, it was not completely successful, however. Despite Goebbels' efforts, morale continued to decline after 1943.

German defeat

Revised

Germany in 1945

By 1945, the Germans had lost the war. The Soviets, who had inflicted a series of defeats upon the Germans in Eastern Europe in late 1944, reached the border of Germany at the Oder River on 23 January. The US army crossed the **Rhine** on 7 March 1945 and met the Soviets at the **Elbe** on 25 April, as the Soviets closed in on Berlin. Despite inevitable German defeat, the Nazis did not surrender and the Battle of Berlin was the largest of the war. On 30 April, Hitler committed suicide in his bunker in Berlin after appointing Admiral Doenitz as his replacement. With the Soviets occupying Berlin, Germany, now without a government, finally surrendered on 8 May.

The extent of the defeat, the scale of the conflict and the refusal to surrender until the bitter end left Germany in ruins: Germany had reached **zero hour**. How had Germany been so comprehensively defeated?

Factors in German defeat

- Overstretch: in invading the Soviet Union in 1941 and declaring war on the USA in 1942, Nazi Germany ended up attempting to fight a war against powerful enemies and across several fronts. Germany fought across a huge front line in the Soviet Union, as well as in North Africa and then Italy. At Stalingrad, the German army was thousands of miles from home at the end of a precarious **supply line**. They also had to contend with bombing campaigns against their cities, and then a front in France after D-Day in June 1944.
- The strength of their enemies: Germany's enemies included the world's largest imperial power (Britain), the world's largest economic power (the USA), and the Soviet Union with its vast human and material resources (34 million men served in Soviet armed forces during the war). The USA assisted its Allies through the **Lend Lease scheme**. For example, the Soviet Union received 13,000 tanks from the USA, and Allied success in the Battle of the Atlantic kept Britain supplied. The combined power of the economies and military forces of Germany's enemies was just too great. Germany's allies, such as Italy, were weak: for instance, Italy's failure to maintain its position in North Africa caused the Germans to divert soldiers to fight there.
- A chaotic and inefficient state: Germany did not organise its war effort effectively.
  - Its economy was hampered by disorder and poor co-ordination. The Soviet war economy was more productive and its labour force (particularly women) better mobilised than the German war economy.
  - When Germany went to war in 1939, the Four Year Plan (see page 36) had only equipped the country to fight small conflicts.
  - Nazi Germany's exploitation of raw materials in captured areas was inefficient.
  - The Nazis also wasted energy on ideological campaigns such as the **Holocaust**, rather than focusing exclusively on winning the war.
  - Hitler hampered German military effectiveness with **hubristic** ambitions for Germany, as seen in his decision to invade the USSR.
- Shortages: Nazi Germany failed to capture key resources such as oil in North Africa and the Caucasus. By 1944, the Allies had three times as much oil as Germany. Germany often ran short of vital raw materials and equipment, a key factor leading to its defeat at Stalingrad in 1943.

Introducing an argument

Below are a sample exam-style question, a list of key points to be made in the essay, and a simple introduction and conclusion to the essay. Read the question, the plan, and the introduction and conclusion. Rewrite the introduction and conclusion in order to develop an argument.

To what extent was the defeat of Germany in the Second World War due to the strength of its enemies?

Key points

- The strength of Germany's enemies.
- German overstretch.
- The failures of the German war economy.
- Shortages of raw materials.

Introduction

One reason for German defeat in the Second World War was the strength of their enemies. Other factors include the fact that Germany was overstretched in its war effort, the failures of its war economy, and the shortages of raw materials.

Conclusion

Germany was defeated in the Second World War for a number of reasons. The strength of Germany's enemies was an important factor but not the only one.

You're the examiner

a

Below are a sample exam-style question and a paragraph written in answer to this question. Read the paragraph and the mark scheme provided on page 68. Decide which level you would award the paragraph. Write the level below, along with a justification for your choice.

To what extent did the chaos and inefficiency in the Nazi state contribute to the defeat of Germany in the Second World War?

Chaos and inefficiency in the Nazi state contributed to the defeat of Germany in the Second World War to an extent. The war economy for example was chaotically organised. Various organisations such as the Todt Organisation and the Office of the Four Year Plan had overlapping roles. There was also a lack of co-ordination, so uniform standards for ammunition were only introduced after 1943 under Albert Speer. Gauleiter also often resisted central control and hindered efficiency by running their own economic schemes. There were also inefficiencies in the Nazis' use of the labour force, where they did not fully make use of female labour. The Nazis also did not exploit the resources of countries that they invaded very effectively. All of this made it more difficult for Germany to win the war.

Level: Reason for choosing this level:

Exam focus

Revised

Below is a sample essay that reaches Level 5. Read it and the examiner comments around it.

Why, after a period of initial success, did Nazi Germany lose the war by 1945?

The introduction signals that a range of factors will be considered.

In 1940, Germany appeared to be in a very strong position to win the war. It had overrun Poland, Scandinavia, the Low Countries and France very rapidly, and appeared to be unbeatable. However, by 1945, Nazi Germany was completely defeated and the Soviet Union occupied Berlin. There were a number of reasons for this, perhaps most crucially that Germany became overstretched and its enemies were just too powerful. Chaos and inefficiency within the Nazi state also contributed to its defeat.

The candidate focuses on the reasons why the Nazis were unable to sustain their initial success.

Specific and detailed evidence to support the point.

A very significant reason why Germany lost the Second World War was that, from 1941, it was overstretched in its war effort. Rather than consolidating his early gains, in June 1941 Hitler dramatically escalated the war when he ordered Operation Barbarossa: the invasion of the Soviet Union. Initially this attack seemed to be very successful. However, in taking on the Soviet Union, Hitler had significantly increased the chance that Germany would lose the war. The Soviet Union was a huge country with a great many resources and an enormous army, all of which made it more likely that the Germans would lose. Ultimately, the Soviets were able to deploy 34 million men to fight in the war. By invading the Soviet Union, the German army ended up a very long way away from home, at the end of precarious supply lines, and at Stalingrad, were defeated by superior Soviet forces. Whilst fighting in the Soviet Union, Nazi Germany was also attempting to fight in North Africa: its forces and resources became overstretched and made German defeat more likely. In this way, Germany lost the war because, instead of consolidating early victories, Hitler attacked the Soviet Union, bringing a powerful enemy into the war.

Factors are linked together. It is good practice to consider how various causes relate to one another.

German overstretch combined with the strength of Germany's enemies to make German defeat more likely. In addition to fighting Britain, the world's largest imperial power, and the Soviet Union, Nazi Germany declared war on the USA after Pearl Harbor in December 1941. Germany's enemies had enormous combined strength and were able to assist each other to ensure German defeat. So, for example, the American Lend Lease scheme supplied the Soviets and the British with equipment. The Soviets received 13,000 tanks from the USA through this scheme. American soldiers also assisted with victory of Nazi forces in Italy, and Britain and the USA worked together in the Battle of the Atlantic. Early victories had been based on the relative superiority of Germany's forces. However, from 1941, Germany was too weak to win the war because of the combined strength of its enemies.

The paragraph concludes by explaining why the Nazis' initial successes turned to defeat, thus focusing on the precise wording of the question.

In addition, chaos and inefficiency in the Nazi economy also hindered the Nazi war effort and contributed to their defeat. In the short term, against France and Poland, the chaos did not stop early successes. However, in the long term the Nazis' chaotic war economy could not manage to produce as much as their enemies. Albert Speer did improve things after 1943, and ammunitions production rose by 97 per cent. However, by this time Germany was competing with the economies of the Soviet Union, the USA and Britain. Moreover, the state was never able to organise other aspects of its war effort efficiently. So, for example, ideology caused the Nazis to waste energy on pursuing the Holocaust, and Hitler refused to mobilise women because of his belief that they should not work. In addition, the Nazis did not use the resources of countries that they invaded well. In this way Germany lost the war because its economy was too chaotic and, compared to its enemies, too weak to sustain its early success.

Overall, Germany was defeated by 1945 for a number of reasons. Its early successes were based on its strength compared to its enemies. However, rather than consolidate his early gains, Hitler invaded the Soviet Union and declared war on the USA. Therefore, Germany took on too much and its enemies were too powerful. What is more, the inefficiencies of the Nazi war economy meant that in the long term Germany was unable to sustain its advantage, and therefore in spite of its initial success Germany lost the war.

The argument that was advanced at the start is restated here. High-graded candidates will try to sustain their arguments.

28/30

This is a well-written essay which contains a sustained argument. A range of points are considered, and points are supported by a lot of precise evidence and examples. It also focuses on the change in Germany's fortunes and therefore focuses on the precise wording of the question. Therefore, due to its precise focus, its sustained analysis and the amount of supporting detail it gains a high mark in Level 5.

What makes a good answer?

You have now considered four sample A-grade essays. Use these essays to make a bullet-pointed list of the characteristics of an A-grade essay. Use this list when planning and writing your own practice exam essays.

Timeline

1918 Outbreak of revolution in Germany.

Abdication of Kaiser Wilhelm II.

Declaration of the Weimar Republic.

Ebert–Groener Pact.

Armistice.

1919 Ebert elected president.

Spartacist uprising.

Weimar constitution adopted.

Treaty of Versailles signed.

1920 Kapp Putsch.

Support for pro-Weimar parties slumps to 45 per cent.

1921 Hitler becomes Führer of the Nazi Party.

1923 Hyperinflation crisis.

Munich Putsch.

1924 Dawes Plan.

1925 Hindenburg elected president.

1926 Germany admitted into the League of Nations.

1928 Reichstag election: 76 per cent of voters support pro-Weimar parties; the Nazis gain 2.6 per cent of the vote.

1929 The Young Plan.

The Wall Street Crash.

1932 Hindenburg wins the presidential election.

Nazis gain 37 per cent of the vote in the Reichstag election in July, becoming the largest party in the Reichstag.

1933 Hitler appointed chancellor.

The Enabling Act is passed.

Boycott of Jewish shops.

All political parties, except for the Nazis, disbanded.

1935 Nuremburg Laws passed.

1936 Creation of the Four Year Plan organisation.

1938 Kristallnacht.

1939 Reich Central Office for Emigration established.

German invasion of Poland and the start of the Second World War.

Start of the Aktion T4 programme.

1940 Battle of Britain.

1941 Operation Barbarossa – the German invasion of the Soviet Union.

Systematic massacre of Jews in the Soviet Union begins.

1942 Wannsee Conference.

Speer appointed Minister for Munitions.

1943 Allies bomb Hamburg.

1944 D-Day.

1945 Allies bomb Dresden.

Hitler commits suicide.

End of the Second World War.

Glossary

Absenteeism Absence from work for reasons other than sickness.

Aktion T4 The Nazis' programme dealing with the euthanasia or murder of disabled children and adults.

The Allies In the context of the First World War: Britain, Russia and France and their empires. In the context of the Second World War: Britain and France and their empires, later joined by the USSR and USA.

Anschluss The union of Germany and Austria.

Anti-Semitism Prejudiced views or hatred towards Jewish people or the Jewish religion or measures that discriminate against Jews.

Appeasement Attempting to resolve a dispute by making concessions to an aggressor in order to avoid war.

Aristocratic elite A social group who have inherited their wealth and status.

Armistice An agreement to stop fighting at the end of a war.

Autarkic A description of an economy which seeks to be self-sufficient and not depend upon impacts or foreign loans.

Autocratic Refers to a system of government entailing the rule of one person: an autocrat is a ruler of a country who holds all power.

Autobahns German motorways.

Aryans A supposed racial group of northern Europeans often associated with blond hair, blue eyes and physical strength.

Aryan racial supremacy A racist ideology which conceives of 'Aryans' as superior.

Balance of payments The difference between how much a country's economy imports and how much it exports.

The Bamberg Conference A Nazi Party conference in 1926 at which Hitler's role as the single all-powerful leader of the movement was reinforced. In addition, Hitler defeated the left of the party to ensure that the Nazi Party had a clearly right-wing agenda.

Bargaining power The power that workers have to negotiate their pay levels and conditions at work.

The Battle of the Atlantic A battle in the Second World War between the German navy and the Allies' navies and air forces.

The Battle of Britain An air battle between Britain and Germany in 1940. German and British fighter pilots fought in the skies above southern England. Hitler's aim was to try to force the British out of the war: he did not succeed in this.

Bauhaus A modern school of design founded in Germany in 1919.

Beauty of Labour A Nazi scheme to improve the physical appearance of workplaces.

Bilateral An agreement between two countries.

Blitzkreig Literally: 'lightning war': the tactics of the German army when invading in the Second World War.

'Blood and Soil' A Nazi belief in the importance of bloodline and land to national identity.

Burgfrieden A term used by Kaiser Wilhelm II at the start of the First World War to mean 'national truce': a term for unity in the German political scene at the start of the war.

Cabaret A sometimes satirical art form practised in nightclubs usually through the medium of dance and song.

Checks and balances Parts of a constitution or political system that ensure that no one part of the system or individual within it can have excessive power.

Civil rights individual rights, such as freedom of speech or freedom from arbitrary arrest.

Collateral Something used to guarantee security, for example, for a loan or currency. For instance, gold to guarantee paper money; property as collateral for a loan.

Concentration camp (In Nazi Germany) Camps where the Nazis held their opponents or others, such as racial minorities, who did not fit into their ideal for society. Conditions in camps were usually poor.

Conscription Compulsory enlistment into the army.

Conservative/s People or political movements who favour upholding traditional institutions, values and social classes.

Constitution The basic set of rules that govern the political system of a country.

Coup The forced seizure of power by a group, often the army.

Dambusters The name given to the 1942 air raid on industrial targets in the Ruhr. The key target was a dam.

DAP (German Worker's Party) Founded by Anton Drexler in 1919, it was one of many small extreme nationalist parties that emerged following

German defeat in the First World War. The name of the party reflected Drexler's ambition to gain support from German workers for his nationalist aims. Hitler Joined the party in 1919 and soon became its leading figure. The DAP was renamed the National Socialist German Workers' Party in February 1920.

D-Day The Allied invasion of Normandy in France on 6 June 1944. The invasion opened up a third front against the Nazis in Europe.

DDP The German Democratic Party. A centrist pro-Democratic party.

Death squads Organised groups that murdered people on political grounds.

Decadence A culture of frivolity and indulgence. Decadence usually implies moral decline.

Decree An official order or law.

Demilitarised Removing or not allowing a military force from an area, for example, the Rhineland after the First World War.

Dissolve (In the context of a parliament) To remove all members of a parliamentary body from their posts. Usually a new election is then called.

DNVP The German National People's Party. A right-wing, generally anti-democratic party that sometimes co-operated with the Nazis. The DNVP was also associated with President Hindenburg.

DVP German People's Party. This party started as a nationalistic, anti-Weimar right-wing party but became pro-Weimar and more moderate by the early 1920s.

Eastern Front (In the First and Second World Wars) The front line between German/German–Austrian forces and Russian/Soviet forces.

Edelweiss Pirates An illegal youth group in Nazi Germany which was opposed to Nazi rule.

The Elbe A river in Germany.

Einsatzgruppen SS death squads which followed the German army as Germany conquered eastern Europe and the Soviet Union carrying out mass killings of ideological and 'racial' enemies of the Nazis.

Entrenched Something that is stable and secure.

Ersatz Substitute or replacement goods.

Eugenics The pseudo-scientific study of genetics in which doctors and scientists sought to 'improve' the genetic characteristics of the human race through breeding or restriction on breeding.

Expressionist Artistic works in which artists seek to reveal their personal emotional responses through, for example, use of vivid colour or exaggerated perspective.

Federal A system where a great deal of political level rests at local or regional level.

The Final Solution The euphemistic term the Nazis used to refer to the Holocaust and death camps: they were, in Nazi terms, the 'final solution to the Jewish question'.

Four Year Plan The Nazi economic plan from 1936. The plan focused upon building a war economy.

Freedom of association The freedom to form organisations with others, for instance, religious groups or trades unions.

Freikorps Paramilitary (informal) groups of volunteer soldiers. In inter-war Germany these groups were often strongly nationalist and linked to extremist politics.

Front An area of combat in a war.

Führerprinzip The principle that within the Nazi Party Hitler possessed all power and authority. The *Führerprinzip* later became the operating principle for the Nazi state when Hitler was in power.

Gauleiter Regional Nazi Party leaders who, after the party came to power, became regional political leaders.

Genocide The systematic destruction of a people or a culture.

Gold mark The gold version of the German currency.

The Grand Coalition The 1928–1932 coalition government, led by Müller and containing representatives of left, right and centre. The government, which had the support of 65 per cent of the Reichstag, seemed to herald a new and more stable era for German politics. The coalition fell apart, however, in failing to agree on measures to tackle the Depression.

The Great Depression The world-wide economic depression which occurred after the Wall Street Crash in 1929 and lasted until the mid 1930s. An economic depression is a prolonged period of stagnation characterised by shrinking or stagnant economies and rising unemployment.

Hitler Salute A straight-armed salute given to show support for Hitler.

The Holocaust The Nazis' systematic murder of Jews and other groups throughout Europe, such as Roma or Sinti, 1939–1945.

Hubristic Arrogant, over-confident.

Indoctrinated Brainwashed: persuaded through propaganda or manipulation to believe in a set of ideas.

Inflation When prices rise and the amount that can be purchased with each unit of a currency reduces: the value of a currency declines.

Isolationist A policy in which a country avoids involvement in foreign affairs.

Judiciary Judges.

Junker class The old elite of Germany; the dominant social group in the Second Reich. Junkers were aristocratic landowners from Prussia who occupied most of the senior positions in the army, civil service and politics in the Second Reich.

The Kapp Putsch An attempt to take over the government of the Weimar Republic by a group of right-wing nationalists and supporters of the *Freikorps*.

KPD The German Communist Party.

Kristallnacht The 'Night of Broken Glass': the Nazi attacks on Jewish property and businesses on the night of 9–10 November 1938.

Labour exchanges Offices where the unemployed go to seek work and employers advertise vacancies.

The League of Nations An international organisation formed in the aftermath of the First World War to promote peace and international co-operation.

Lebensraum 'Living space'. The idea that Germany needed extra land to thrive: in other words it should take over lands in eastern Europe.

Left wing Political beliefs that promote the creation of a more equal society.

Legislation Laws.

Lend Lease scheme The scheme under which the United States supplied or loaned its Allies equipment and materials to assist with the war effort during the Second World War.

Lobbying Attempts to convince a political figure or movement of the merits of a cause or argument.

The Low Countries Belgium, Holland and Luxembourg.

Luftwaffe The German air force during the Nazi era.

The mark A unit of German currency at this time.

Mefo Bills A kind of substitute currency with which the Nazi government paid for investment and government projects. Mefo Bills could be exchanged for actual currency after four years. They allowed the government to spend money in the short term without having to borrow money or raise taxes.

Minority administrations Governments that only have the support of a minority in parliament.

Mobilised Organised for war.

The Munich Putsch The attempt by the Nazi Party in November 1923 to seize power and start a national revolution against Weimar democracy.

Nationalist A political idea that seeks to glorify the nation.

Nazi–Soviet Pact The agreement of August 1939 between Nazi Germany and the USSR in which the USSR agreed not to attack Nazi Germany if it were to attack Poland, and the two countries agreed that in the event of a Nazi attack on Poland, they would divide the country between them.

The New Plan Schacht's 1934 economic plan.

Non-conformity Not fitting in with society's normal values.

The Nuremburg Laws The Nazis' racist 1935 laws that removed German citizenship from Jews, banned inter-marriage between Jews and other Germans and defined who was to be considered Jewish.

Operation Barbarossa The German name for its invasion of the USSR in 1941.

Operation Bagration A huge Soviet military offensive in 1944 in eastern Europe.

Oratory The skill of speech-making.

Passive resistance Resisting a government and/or state via peaceful (though not necessarily legal) means.

Patronage The power to be able to appoint or dismiss people from positions.

Pearl Harbor A US naval base in the Pacific attacked by Japan in December 1941.

Phoney war Where a war has been declared but no fighting occurs.

Plenipotentiary A person who has full powers over an area of policy, for example, Goering in the office of the Four Year Plan.

Polarised/polarisation In a political context this means a process whereby the political scene divides between the extreme left and the extreme right.

Proportional representation An electoral system in which seats allocated in parliament correspond exactly or very closely to the way in which people vote, i.e. if 10 per cent of voters vote for a party, then that party receives 10 per cent of the seats in parliament.

Prussia A powerful, historic German state.

Putsch An attempt to seize power.

The Red Army The army of the Soviet Union.

Referendum A democratic vote on a single issue. It can also be called a plebiscite.

Reflationary schemes Schemes to try to get a shrinking economy growing again by getting more money into the economy.

Reich Food Estate The Nazi state's organisation that regulated food production and distribution.

Reichstag The German parliament.

Reichsrat (In the Second Reich) The second chamber of the German parliament. The Reichsrat represented the states of Germany.

The Rentenmark A new currency introduced temporarily in Germany in 1923 to replace the hyper-inflated currency.

The Rhine A river that runs through Germany.

The Rot Kappelle A Communist anti-Nazi group in the 1930s.

***Schutzstaffel* (SS)** This organisation started off in 1920 as Hitler's personal bodyguard but expanded to become the main agent of terror in Nazi Germany. The SS was fiercely loyal to Hitler and his ideas. By 1934, the SS was rival to the SA as the primary enforcer of Nazism. The SS was led by Heinrich Himmler and was responsible for repression and death camps in occupied territories in eastern Europe during the Second World War.

Scorched earth policy A policy by which an advancing or retreating army or political power destroys land and infrastructure in their wake.

Siegfried 'Victory peace': a victorious war of conquest.

Socialist A political ideology which advocates greater equality in society and the collective ownership of property and industry.

Social revolution A revolution that changes the social structure, that is the class basis, of society.

SOPADE The SPD in exile.

Soviets Workers' councils, that is, workers' organisations which run their own workplaces.

The Soviet Union A Russian-dominated Communist state in eastern Europe and Asia.

Spartacist League A communist-affiliated political group in the Weimar Republic. Spartacists placed greater weight on the need for revolutions to have popular support than did Lenin, communist leader of the Soviet Union.

Spanish flu pandemic A devastating outbreak of flu that hit the world after the First World War causing up to 50 million deaths.

SPD The Social Democratic Party of Germany. The main left-wing political party in Germany.

Sportpalast A large sports centre in Berlin.

Star of David A symbol of the Jewish religion.

'Stab in the Back' myth The right-wing myth that Germany only lost the First World War because of the revolution of autumn 1918 and because it was betrayed by socialists, communists, liberals and Jews. In reality, Germany had already essentially lost the war before the revolution occurred.

Stock market crash A collapse in the price of shares in a stock market. The Wall Street Crash is the name given to the crash of the US stock markets, based in Wall Street, New York, that started in October 1929.

Strength Through Joy A Nazi organisation that promoted leisure opportunities for workers.

***Sturmabteilung* (SA)** The Brownshirts. Nazi storm troopers.

Supply line A route by which supplies to an army are passed.

The Swing Youth Groups of young people in Nazi Germany who did not conform to Nazi ideals in their style of dress, parties, and preference for listening to American Jazz.

The Todt Organisation A Nazi economic organisation during the Second World War.

Universal suffrage Everyone having the vote.

USPD The independent Social Democratic Party of Germany – a breakaway political party from the SPD who were to its left.

The USSR The Union of Soviet Socialist Republics: the official name for the Soviet Union (see above).

V1 and V2 German rockets during the Second World War.

Volksgemeinschaft A national or people's community.

Waffen SS A militarised part of the SS responsible for a great many atrocities during the Second World War.

War bonds Bought by citizens or businesses during wartime from the government to assist with the costs of the war: in effect, people lend the government money.

The *Wehrmacht* The German army before 1945.

Wehrwirtschaft A war economy.

Working class A social group that does not possess assets or capital and whose economic basis is the sale of its labour.

Zero hour A term used to describe the low point that Germany had reached by the end of the Second World War. Germany was defeated and devastated.

Answers

Section 1: The fall of the Second Reich and the creation of Weimar Germany

Page 5, Complete the paragraph: suggested answer

To some extent the main impact of the First World War was the political problems the war produced. The war increased tensions as many people disliked the 'silent dictatorship' of Ludendorff and Hindenburg. These generals effectively ran the country from 1916, and their authoritarian leadership produced opposition. Huge strikes in 1917 and 1918 show the extent of people's discontent. As the war dragged on, politics became more divided. The Reichstag opposed the government by urging them to try to negotiate a peace settlement in 1917, whilst the Spartacists and the USPD were completely anti-war. Politics was polarised as the generals continued to seek a Siegfried. **The political polarisation that the war produced in Germany caused made political divisions in the country harder to resolve, increased opposition to the political system and made revolution more likely. For these reasons the political tensions caused by the First World War had a very significant impact on Germany.**

Page 7, Delete as applicable

The Second Reich collapsed **mainly** because of the impact of the First World War. The war placed enormous strains on Germany that made revolution **certain**. For example, the cost of fighting the war led to inflation: the mark declined in value by 75 per cent during the war. Inflation and shortages reduced living standards, increased ordinary people's discontent, and made revolution more likely. In addition, the war increased political tension, with some groups such as the Spartacists and USPD party opposed to Germany continuing to fight in the war. The difficulties that fighting in the First World War produced **mainly** caused the Second Reich to collapse because **they led to major economic problems which, in turn led to a political revolution.**

Page 7, Eliminate irrelevance

It is unlikely that the Second Reich would have collapsed if Germany had not been losing the First World War in autumn 1918. The revolution, which caused the Kaiser to flee and the Reich to end, was triggered by a mutiny by sailors in Kiel. ~~The Kaiser was the supreme ruler of Germany. He took over ruling Germany in 1888 and he was very interested in ships~~. The sailors rebelled because they were aware that Germany was on the verge of losing the war. The political changes that had started right before the revolution were also caused by Germany losing the war, as it was this knowledge that caused the generals who were running the country to hand over power to a new government that was backed by the Reichstag. While there were underlying problems and conflicts in the Second Reich that made revolution more likely, it is still unlikely that the system would have collapsed if Germany had won the First World War.

Page 9, Spot the mistake

This paragraph does not get into Level 4 for AO1 because the material is generalised and undeveloped. More explanation and specific examples would improve it.

Page 11, Develop the detail

It is not accurate to say that the Treaty of Versailles was mainly responsible for the political and economic instability in Germany in the years 1919–1923. The Treaty of Versailles did contribute, however, to political and economic instability in the country at this time. The Treaty contained many aspects that people in Germany did not like and this helped extremists in Germany to gain support: Germans regarded the Treaty as a *diktat*, **or dictated peace. In addition, the imposition of restrictions on the German military, such as the limiting of the size of the army to 100,000 soldiers, was also disliked, as was the 'War Guilt' clause. Most Germans did not feel that they alone were responsible for the war.** Dislike of the Treaty of Versailles reduced many people's support for the Weimar system **as many people associated its signing with Treaty with Weimar politicians**. In addition, the payment of reparations that the Treaty entailed added to the inflation that Germany had, and this increased economic instability**: the reparations were set at £6600 million in 1921 and the requirement to pay them added to inflation. Overall, the Treaty of Versailles was not the main cause of political and economic instability in Germany in the years 1919–1923, but it did add to the problems that Germany faced.**

Page 15, Turning assertion into argument: suggested answer

Political extremists were a major threat to the stability of the Weimar Republic because **they tried to overthrow the whole system of government in putsches and attempted revolutions**

such as in the Kapp Putsch of 1920 and the Spartacist Uprising of 1919. In addition, political extremists destabilised the Republic in the years 1919–1923 through their use of political violence and murder which created an atmosphere of fear and instability.

The legacy of the First World War was also a threat to the stability of the Weimar Republic in the sense that **people associated the Republic with the defeat from which it was born and the humiliation of the Treaty of Versailles: these negative associations reduced people's support for Weimar and thus undermined its stability.**

Economic problems such as inflation were also a threat to the stability of the Weimar Republic in that **inflation was a significant problem by 1922 and by 1923 hyperinflation existed. People's savings and income were rendered worthless and this destabilised Weimar's economy.**

Page 17, You're the examiner

The paragraph should be awarded a mark in Level 4 as it shows clear focus on the question and provides accurate, relevant and detailed supporting evidence.

Page 21, Identify an argument

Sample 2 contains the argument.

Section 2: The rise of the Third Reich

Page 25, Spot the mistake

The paragraph does not get into AO1, Level 4 because the link between what is written and the question is not clear enough: more explanation is needed.

Page 27, Eliminate irrelevance

The changes that the Nazi Party made in the 1920s account for the Party's increased popularity after 1928 to a limited extent. The improved structure helped the Party in election campaigns. Hitler established a national network of Party organisations headed up by regional Party leaders, the *Gauleiter*. The local Nazi Party organisations helped to publicise the Party and increase its popularity, and assisted in running election campaigns which helped to increase the Nasis' share of the vote. A number of Nazi organisations were established in the 1920s which later helped draw people into the movement. The Hitler Youth was one of these. ~~After Hitler came to power the Hitler Youth became compulsory and during the Second World War some members even ended up fighting for the Nazis~~. These measures helped to increase Nazi Party popularity by enabling improved campaigning and by drawing more people into the movement.

Page 29, Turning assertion into argument

The high level of unemployment in Germany 1930–1932 helped Hitler come to power because **many of the unemployed believed that the economic problems showed that democracy had failed and therefore they were willing to support Hitler's Nazi alternative.**

The failure of Brüning, von Papen and von Schleicher's governments to gain the support of the Reichstag helped Hitler come to power in the sense that **it persuaded von Papen and Hindenburg that, having tried all the alternatives, they had little choice but to do a deal with Hitler.**

The failure of politicians to come up with effective solutions to the 1930s Depression helped Hitler to gain power **because it allowed Hitler to claim that traditional politics had failed and therefore Germany should embrace his new radical alternative.**

Page 31, Develop the detail

The electoral success of the Nazi Party helped Hitler come to power in the sense that it made him a candidate to become chancellor. The Nazi Party's support grew substantially between the 1928 and the 1932 elections. **In 1928, the Party only obtained 2.6 per cent of the vote, whilst by July 1932 it received 37.3 per cent and 230 seats in the Reichstag. The Party was by this time the most popular in Germany and the largest in the Reichstag. The effective propaganda campaigns deployed by Goebbels, along with the ongoing political and economic crisis in Germany, helped the Party gain in elections.** The Party picked up support from people**, such as conservative women,** who did not like the Weimar Republic and this popularity **and success in elections** made Hitler a candidate to be chancellor.

Page 31, Identify an argument

Sample 1 contains the argument.

Page 33, You're the examiner

The paragraph should be awarded Level 3 because it makes a point that is focused on the question and backs this up with some detail. For Level 4 the paragraph should be developed with more depth and analysis to explain the role of the factor in Hitler's appointment.

Section 3: The Third Reich in action

Page 37, Identify an argument

Sample 1 contains the argument.

Page 39, Develop the detail

The Nazis were partially successful in creating a *Volksgemeinschaft*. One way in which the Nazis tried to do this was through introducing policies to appeal to different social groups. So, for example, there were policies to appeal to the working class and to peasants and farmers. **Policies that benefited some in the working class included the KdF, Strength through Joy scheme that promoted leisure opportunities for workers, most famously cruises in the Baltic. In addition, some of the Nazis' family policies benefited poorer families. Furthermore, peasants and farmers benefited from tariffs that helped to protect prices and from schemes to write off debts.** These policies **encouraged people to support the Nazis and** contributed to the Nazis' partial success in creating a *Volksgemeinschaft*.

Page 45, Delete as applicable

In terms of education, the lives of young people in Germany 1933–1939 changed **to a great extent**. In schools, the curriculum was heavily controlled by the Nazis after 1935 and all textbooks had to be approved by the Nazis. The Nazis used education as a means of spreading their ideology, and so for example, their racial theories were taught in biology, and anti-Semitic ideas were promoted. Nazi ideology about the roles of men and women was also promoted, as was a nationalistic view of German history. In addition, the Nazis removed teachers who were considered to be politically hostile to them from schools to try to control what students were being taught. The Nazis' educational policies had a **significant impact** on young people in Nazi Germany in the sense that **they changed the focus of education so that young people were more likely to support the Nazis.**

Page 45, You're the examiner

This is a Level 3 answer as although it focuses on the question and contains some detail, it does not end with analysis.

Section 4: The fall of the Third Reich

Page 51, Complete the paragraph: suggested answer

The failings of Nazi economic policies contributed to some extent to the defeat of Germany in the Second World War. There was often a lack of effective co-ordination in the war economy and the actions of *Gauleiter* often worked against economic efficiency. In addition, the Nazis relied heavily upon foreign workers, of whom there were 6.4 million by 1942. Foreign workers were often underfed, badly treated and their productivity was low: 60–80 per cent less than that of the average German worker. Furthermore, because of Nazi ideology woman were not always effectively mobilised. **The failures of these aspects of Nazi economic policy contributed to some extent to the defeat of Germany in the Second World War because they resulted in the Nazis being out-produced by their rivals which was a major hindrance to German victory.**

Page 53, Identify an argument

Sample 2 contains the argument.

Page 55, Delete as applicable

German defeat in the Second World War was **partly** due to the impact of Allied bombing campaigns. Air raids did hinder the German war effort by destroying buildings and infrastructure, such as during Operation Chastise in 1943. Military and industrial sites were targeted. In addition, the bombing campaigns hindered the German war effort through the damage to morale that some of the bombing raids targeted at civilians caused. Around 1 million people were killed and injured in these raids. However, Allied bombing campaigns did not deliver a decisive blow against Germany: they contributed **partly** to German defeat in the sense that **they disrupted war production and undermined civilian morale therefore weakening the German home front.**

Page 55, Develop the detail: suggested answer

Propaganda helped to maintain morale in Germany during the Second World War to some extent. The Nazis used propaganda for this purpose and Goebbels produced a number of films, **such as Kolberg (1943),** with a patriotic message. After 1943, Goebbels redoubled his propaganda efforts and urged Germans to fight on in a famous speech **at the Sportspalast in Berlin where he called for a 'total war' effort**. Whilst propaganda did help the Nazis to maintain morale, it was not completely successful, however. Despite Goebbels' efforts, morale continued to decline after 1943: **there is evidence that many in the Hitler Youth were dissatisfied after this point for example. Defeats in the war, shortages and conditions at work all contributed to declining morale after this date.**

Page 57, You're the examiner

This is a Level 3 answer as although it focuses on the question and contains some detail, it ends with an assertion rather than analysis.

Mark scheme

For some of the activities in the book it will be useful to refer to the mark scheme for the unit. Below is the mark scheme for Unit 1.

Level	Marks	Description
1	1–6	• Lacks focus on the question. • Limited factual accuracy. • Highly generalised. *Level 1 answers are highly simplistic, irrelevant or vague.*
2	7–12	• General points with some focus on the question. • Some accurate and relevant supporting evidence. *Level 2 answers might tell the story without addressing the question, or address the question without providing supporting examples.*
3	13–18	• General points that focus on the question. • Accurate support, but this may be either only partly relevant or lacking detail, or both. • Attempted analysis. *Level 3 answers attempt to focus on the question, but have significant areas of weakness. For example, the focus on the question may drift, the answer may lack specific examples, or parts of the essay may simply tell the story. Answers that do not deal with factors that are stated in the question cannot achieve higher than Level 3.*
4	19–24	• General points that clearly focus on the question and show understanding of the most important factors involved. • Accurate, relevant and detailed supporting evidence. • Analysis. *Level 4 answers clearly attempt to answer the question and demonstrate a detailed and wide-ranging knowledge of the period studied.*
5	25–30	• As Level 4. • Sustained analysis. *Level 5 answers are thorough and detailed. They clearly engage with the question and offer a balanced and carefully reasoned argument, which is sustained throughout the essay.*

Notes

Notes